THE
EGO
CONTINUUM

THE EGO CONTINUUM

A HOW-TO GUIDE FOR **SHITTY LEADERS** TO BECOME
LESS SHITTY THROUGH **ACTIVE LEADERSHIP**

MARK ROBINSON

PEACH ELEPHANT PRESS

This book is designed to provide information that the author believes to be accurate on the subject matter it covers, and is written from the author's personal experience. In the text that follows, many people's and company's names and identifying characteristics have been changed, so far that any resemblance to actual persons, living or dead, events, companies or locales is entirely coincidental.

THE EGO CONTINUUM is a registered trademark of Mark Robinson.

Copyright © 2017 by Mark Robinson
All rights reserved. This book or any portion thereof may not be reproduced or used in any manner whatsoever without the express written permission of the publisher or author except for the use of brief quotations in a book review.

Illustrations by Tom Davidson and are not to be reproduced without the consent of the publisher.

First Printing, 2017

Peach Elephant Press
NonFictionBook.co

CONTENTS

Acknowledgments	ix
First & Foremost	1
Introduction	3

THE BASICS — 15

Active Leadership	17
Learn How to Inspire	26
How to Deliver Feedback Based on the Receiver	34

THE PEOPLE AND THEIR FEELINGS — 43

How to Lead Individuals Individually	45
Catch Your Staff Doing Things Right	58
Feedback Is Not an F-Word	66

THE FINE PRINT   73

Why Your Staff Quit	75
How to Build Your Leadership Brand	83
The Most Missed Leadership Behaviour	94
The Importance of Honesty	97
Trust & Integrity	104

THE INTEGRATION   109

You Don't Have to Like Me (and I Don't Have to Like You)	111
What Demanding Respect Gets You	117
The Ego Continuum	120
Insights into Your Ego Continuum	145
Your Leadership Epitaph	151
Your Corporate Culture	156

ACKNOWLEDGMENTS

I HAVE BEEN ABSOLUTELY BLESSED IN MY LIFE AND CAREER to have some of the most incredible women on this planet mentor, influence or inspire me. Their guidance, support, truth, perseverance and resilience have been an invaluable part of my personal growth and development. And most have no clue. Each of them, whether it was during my childhood or in recent times, have influenced something in me in some way and some time. These influences are what I will share with you in the following pages.

I have reflected immensely during the writing of this book. It has been a historical glance at many years of shitty leadership, shitty behaviours or just a shitty day. These reflective times have been awe-inspiring, and have reminded me of my growth and development, laughter and most importantly, self-forgiveness. I am eternally grateful for it all.

Thank you for the generosity of your time, the efforts you've made over the years, and the direct, or more often indirect, lessons you have taught me.

Reminders:

At any age, one can reflect a character of authenticity.

One must accept one's own mortality and die with grace and dignity, by one's own rules and terms.

At times, I also need talking off the ledge and a trusted vent.

You believed in my skills and abilities during times when I didn't.

You accepted a fancy-pants confused little boy as your friend, without question.

You accepted feedback and allowed me to become less of a shitty leader.

Thank you!

To:

Adrianne Fagan-Pittman
Alyssa Robinson
Anne-Marie Hubbard
Anne-Marie McMaster
Betty Mills
Carrie Warner
Ferne Robinson
Grace Baba-Hoang
Helen Smith
Jackie Nicol
Jane Plumb-Pearlman
Justine MacKay
Kaari Carvalho-Pitts
Kaitlyn Coulter
Kelly Herbert
Laura Reed Foster
Lillian Laufman
Lynn Givens
Patricia Dunwoody
Patricia McCord
Shari Robinson-Coulter
Tracey Sherman-Firestone
Vanessa Lynch
Victoria Morrison
Tanya White
Anne Wood

FIRST & FOREMOST

Why is the word "shitty" used in the sub-title? Isn't that rude or offensive? For some, it could be, but hopefully, through your choice, the word choice intrigues you or makes you curious enough to read this book.

Throughout my career, I have worked with and for some shitty leaders. These are **not** shitty people. There is a vast difference, and I would like to share my perspective.

Effective leadership is a series of behavioural choices. When you engage the correct choices with the right audience, you will create a lasting impact that improves both performance and culture. It's about being aware and choosing the right behaviours with the right people to help induce the right actions in them. It's self-awareness and engagement at its finest. It's asking, *what do I need to demonstrate to help get the best out of you?*

When a leader gets it wrong or doesn't engage, that doesn't label them as a shitty person. It does, however, through my wicked humour, label them as shitty leaders. This journey is about self-discovery into your behaviours; it's about helping you create your how-to guide to help you adopt the right behaviours at the right time. Following this guide will help you become less of a shitty leader. Except if on the off-chance, you're just a shitty person, well, that's a different book and not covered here. So, now that you're no longer offended, happy reading.

INTRODUCTION

"Leaders don't create followers, they create more leaders."
— *Tom Peters*

OF COURSE, I WOULD GET THE JOB; I WORKED FOR a recruitment agency, interviews were my life! This particular job I was applying for was at a company that used my recruitment agency to hire all their employees; I was normally the one directing interviews for them! I dressed up, walked in, and I was as cocky as one could be. People love confidence, right? I came with a presentation I had put together of how one should be leading a team of individuals. On every other slide of my slick PowerPoint presentation (PowerPoint was cool back then, okay?) I had inspirational quotes. It was cheesy and overdone, and I was overconfident.

I'm quite sure that the content in the PowerPoint was overkill; it was a lot of fluff, without much substance. I'm sure there were plenty of spelling mistakes. I am positive now that I made a fool of myself, but back then, I walked out of that interview thinking I had the job in the bag. Meanwhile, they were undoubtedly in the office thinking, "Wow, what was that?" while having a good old laugh because I'm sure I came across as a complete narcissist. I'm sure I seemed cheeky and smug, but I didn't mean to. I just thought that was what I needed to be; I hired nearly all the staff in the company, and everybody knew me already.

There was never any humility, no presence of any gratitude for being there. I just thought I knew that I was good, so why were we even bothering to do an interview? Of course, I didn't say that out loud, but I didn't need to for them to read my attitude loud and clear.

This interview was at a contact centre I was already working with, I recruited for them for four months. I was working closely with the manager, who gave me the full autonomy to hire about 200 staff. The manager and I developed a good relationship during that time. Once the recruitment was complete, she wanted me to work with her as a team manager. Part of their hiring process was for me to meet with her and three of my would-be peers—so, three other team managers. The main manager liked me, but that came as no surprise to me. I wanted the job because I felt like it would give me prestige. It was more money than I was earning at that time, and I wanted to leverage it to further my leadership career. I thought I had the position signed and sealed.

As it turned out, the feedback from my interview with the three team managers was not positive. They felt I wasn't the right "fit" for the role. I perceived that they didn't like me. I was quite disappointed to hear this, so it was a great surprise when the main manager overrode their feedback and hired me. When I first started, I felt bitter towards the three team managers because I had chosen to take their feedback personally. I wanted to be better than them. In my mind, I thought they were all shitty leaders because they didn't want to hire me. Instead of trying to figure out why they didn't want to hire me, or what I could have done to improve, I chose to be offended.

The job consisted of about fifteen contact centre agents reporting to me directly. I would hold bi-weekly one-on-ones with them. While they were talking, rather than paying attention to them as I should've been, I'd be on my phone or checking my emails. I was easily distracted and would interrupt them, or I would only be half-listening. I got away with a lot because, even though I was demonstrating shitty behaviours, I was still personable and approachable. People still seemed to like me, even though I wasn't doing that great of a job in my one-on-ones, as I discovered later upon reflection. At the time, though, I thought I was a superstar genius. But, turns out being well liked didn't make me a good team leader; it just made me well liked.

These one-on-ones were of utmost importance, and I was blowing it. Most managers should meet with their team individually, and host a mini-review with them. Some companies suggest once or twice a month, some bi-weekly. In these sessions, you go through the employee's key performance indicators (KPIs), or their stats. In a call centre, you would look at things like average handle time, talk time, or feedback from customers. You might listen to recorded calls together, and through certain criteria, you'd grade the calls to see how they did.

These one-on-one sessions weren't only to assess your employee's statistics and to provide feedback on how to improve (and save your company money in the meantime). They were also a chance for the manager to spend time with their employee. As we get into the insights of this book, if you want to increase your active leadership, ask yourself, *how often is often enough to engage one-on-one with your staff?* And, it's much more than just the frequency. A fundamental of active leadership is that you should be meeting, at a *minimum*, twice a month with your team, and with your folks individually. Meeting with your staff once a month, to me, is not enough. There is more about active leadership to follow.

What did you take away from my first management role example? For me, my shittiness was that I made it all about me and I wasn't engaged in the one-on-ones. I was easily distracted, which others perceived as insincerity, and it eroded trust. I lacked the follow-through and consistency. I was making the leadership facets about me. I was overlooking my staff when I should have been supporting them. My passion and drive were wanting to be right. I wanted to prove the other team managers wrong, that I was better than them. This was my ego in full competition mode. I was demonstrating a holier-than-thou attitude, which created this perception in the first place. My job was all about ticking a box because I *had* to do the one-on-ones. My actions and behaviours made out like I didn't care, and I am sure some of my staff felt it.

Some of my team used to make comments, asking me why I was always on my phone. I would either ignore the question or make up some lame excuse to validate my behaviour. When you're in a one-on-one, you should give your employee your full, undivided attention. Instead, I would read emails while they were talking, only to look up and realise they'd finished what they had to say. I'd have to ask, "I'm sorry what did you say?" That doesn't make your employees feel valued. I wasn't utilising what a one-on-one was supposed to be used for; it was just something I had to get over with before I could clock off.

When I received feedback from other staff, most of them seemed to like me a lot. This was important to me at the time. There were even people on other teams who would say, "Oh, I wish I was on your team." But then I'd go to our monthly management team meetings and the other team managers would be having tough conversations. I'd hear my peers say, "I had to put her on a development plan. I've noticed that her quality hasn't progressed over the last three one-on-ones. Her average handle time is increasing, and her attendance is decreasing. We've talked about it several times together, and I've tried to set things up to help her succeed. She isn't taking the level of accountability and responsibility we've talked about over the last three sessions. Therefore, I've put her on a development plan for the next 90 days to help her improve. Here are all the key elements of the development plan for her..."

My peers were saying all this, while I was there thinking, *wow! I don't do any of that. I never look at my one-on-one sessions from the last time I met with a person, and I never think about their progression.* My self-awareness hit me like a tonne of bricks; I felt awful. There was so much more I could have (and should have) been doing!

I wanted that team manager job for the wrong reasons. I wanted to be in control. I wanted to feel prestigious because I was in a leadership role. I thought being a leader made me better than other people. I thought that there was a power involved that I wanted and figured I would like. I realised within a few months of being in that role that my job was actually to be supportive, to be honest, and to show integrity.

I learned a lot in that job; it was where I first began to understand that competing against others wasn't right, that it felt wrong. I didn't fully realise until much later that I should only ever be competing with myself. Did I have a better day today than I did yesterday? For some reason, as a society, we decided to give arbitrary things importance. She's prettier than me; she's thinner than me. He makes more money than me. He has a bigger house than me. We collectively decided that we should care about those things. In reality, what actually matters is how you feel about you, and if you had a better day than the previous day. Realising and learning that is the first step to releasing the ego.

Thinking back on that whole debacle now, I wonder why the manager hired me even though the team managers all said no. I believe she saw me as a strong leader, as someone who would be good for her team to learn from. She chalked it up to the fact that the other three managers were insecure about my level of confidence and strength. She just assumed that they felt threatened and that they used the fact that they didn't think I'd be a good fit as an excuse not to hire me. Of course, my ego at the time accepted her rationale as fact; I wasn't quite ready to take the plunge into true self-awareness. This was a prime example of not yet knowing what you don't know.

While I would like to think that she was right, in all honesty, I believe that she wasn't always an active leader. I imagine she had the best intentions in wanting to bring me on because she was looking at it from a strategic perspective. She had six or seven direct reports and wanted someone external that offered strength. I think the others just saw my competitive narcissism, recognising that I wouldn't make an excellent team leader. At the time, they were right.

Since that first eye-opening experience I have spent decades working in leadership roles. I progressed with each new company I worked with, from team manager to manager, to director, to vice president, and finally to a consultant. My title, my level of responsibility and my realisation of how uninspiring upper management can be in so many companies advanced. With that, my sense of what shitty leadership looked and felt like also advanced. I saw it in myself, I felt it, and I lived it. I saw how it affected my team and peers. I knew things needed to change.

Today, it's rare that I go into a company and see inspiring leaders that are taking the time to focus on their staff. It is highly unusual to find a large business whose upper management demonstrates active leadership, who inspire specifically and set the tone for their employees to inspire themselves. I've witnessed misperceptions of ineffective communication, where leaders appeared to want to be more right than kind. They want to catch their staff doing something wrong, versus building their confidence by commending a particular improvement or a productive behaviour. In these businesses, self-righteousness appears as true narcissism, where a plethora of negative perceptions run amok as no-one communicates effectively, or from an authentic place. Most companies focus on the customer, and they forget about their employees. That can be a crucial mistake! If you focus on, embrace, and actively lead your employees, they will automatically provide better experiences. Your staff will feel motivated and inspired as a by-product of you providing sincere time and humility. They will come to work with a smile on their face because they feel valued and aligned. What happens to the customer when your employees feel like this?

It sounds so good—do right for your staff, and you will compel them to do right for your clients. So why isn't this infrastructure everywhere? Simply put, to devote funds and time into quality leadership is an investment for a lot of companies. Many businesses consider it as training, and it's the first expense to go when recessions hit. Outside influences financially impact organisations—inflation, in the year of a presidential election, Brexit, disasters like 9/11 strike. Companies will make cuts, and training is often first to go. They consider training as a luxury and not a necessity. That's just an epic fail. Changing how we lead is not 'training'. Manifesting a culture of feedback is a necessity. You will develop a forward thinking approach to doing things differently that will have a lasting change. This will drive consistent behaviours that impact your staff to simply do what is right! Essential.

Staff are sometimes promoted from within. This makes sense. You have the internal process information skills, experience, abilities and knowledge to move into a supervisory role. It's a smart internal progression that creates advancement opportunities for your staff. However, in some instances, promotion into a supervisory role comes with different requirements. New leaders usually don't have a clue how to be effective leaders. Just because you were a strong non-leader, doesn't instantly make you a strong leader. The two have nothing in common, yet most employers set this as their benchmark. It offers no reasonable logic. It's a setup for failure from Day One.

Sure, I'll concede. Some companies have apprentice programs. Some even have simple supervisory courses, but not to the level of engagement that would set someone up to succeed as an active leader should. It's all extremely cookie-cutter. Every action is the same for every staff member; nothing is individualised for them. You must do monthly one-on-ones. You must make sure you follow all aspects of performance management. Any programs that do exist are usually performance management related and can offer a negative tone. They basically teach you how to write someone up when you catch them doing something wrong, and not much else. They equip you only with the knowledge that you need to check to see if your staff are making their KPIs. They teach you that a 'SMART' goal is a clever mnemonic which stands for specific, measurable, attainable, realistic and time-bound. Okay, you're ready for management now too.

Companies typically invest in teaching the performance management principles, including objective setting, annual appraisals and skills matrices. In these trainings, effective feedback delivery is one element that is often missing. What does this even mean and why is it relevant? What about how to *not* take a cookie-cutter approach in how you deliver feedback? Has anyone ever shared how to engage in feedback based on the particular audience? How will you know why it is so important to build relationships? How well do you know how to inspire and motivate? Do you know what your staff want to do? Do you know how to do this while remaining professional? Are you aware of the type of leader you're perceived to be? What do you leave behind when you engage your staff? All of this is what makes the relationship between you and your staff truly engaging. It's the human element of effective leadership which we call 'active leadership'. I've personally witnessed very few workplaces that deploy this. Instead, they create robotic leaders who don't take their staff to the next level, and then wonder why behaviours and ultimately, the culture, never change.

Active leadership from my lens is comprised of three components. Effective feedback delivery is an essential element. We will also delve into leadership brand and self-awareness—two powerful elements that will raise your leadership game to new levels when authentically engaged.

The environment created in companies that churn out robot-sounding leaders instead of active and engaging leaders can be anywhere from uninspiring to toxic. Some call centres, in particular, are known for having poor attrition rates—employees don't stay, they don't last, and it's always just a job to pay the bills. When people are hired, it's a bums-on-seats mentality. It feels like 'hire those you can and sort them out later'. These companies, at some point, end up saturating their hiring market and struggle to find the right people. They continuously hire just to have people leave in 3 months' time because the work environment feels toxic. Suddenly, there's no one left to hire, or their reputation will stop great staff from applying. These companies end up having to take people on that they wouldn't normally choose, who are then entrusted to support your valuable, paying customers.

Furthermore, if you do stay long enough to be promoted into a leadership role, you're expected to direct these typically challenging-to-manage people without having any supervisory training yourself! It creates a toxic, repetitive culture where nothing ever changes. You won't find much autonomy in these companies. The agents don't feel empowered to do what's right. Rather, if they do take some initiative, they would probably not receive the required support or guidance because there's little to no effective communication.

You can avoid all this by simply putting your staff first. Yes, without your customers you don't have a business, but without your employees, you have nobody to manage the customer! The employee is just as important as the client, if not, dare I say it, more important. You need to embrace your staff, find out what motivates them both intrinsically and extrinsically. The team managers should have the autonomy to genuinely focus on their people. The company should make the individuals and feedback their priority.

Sometimes, companies seem to have it backwards: their primary focus is on their bottom line instead of their people. Of course, some would argue that profitability is the most important factor and, in some instances, I don't disagree. Most organisations look at the cost of doing service. They look at customer satisfaction (CSAT) and the proportion of dissatisfied customers (DSAT). There is no arguing that profits are necessary.

However, to maintain those profits and seek a long-term cost-reduction initiative can be directly linked to the sustainability of an effective and actively led workforce. Companies don't take their approach to a deep enough level, which is employee satisfaction (ESAT.) What supportive leadership brand do employers use to support their leaders to be better leaders? How deep do they choose to take the approach and create an embedded environment, where shitty leadership is simply not acceptable? Do they have the right tools to do the job effectively?

If we create a culture of active leadership, everything simplifies as a natural consequence. Right now, most businesses have to focus on bringing eighty percent of their staff up to scratch, while the top twenty percent carry the company. What if we reverse that? Why can't eighty percent of the staff do everything they should be, instead of needing constant reminders of how to demonstrate productive behaviours.

When you work with or for someone that you respect and admire, it is normal for you to want to do your best for that person. Actively lead eight out of your ten staff so that they choose to respect and support you. Make it so that they feel as if you care about them and that they are valued so that when they have a bad customer experience, it won't be the end of the world. Give specific attention to each one of those eight staff on what they need for them to feel engaged and supported in their role. This way they will know their manager has their back, and that if they need a five-minute vent, they can do so without fear of repercussion. Sometimes we just have a bad moment and need reassurance that everything will be okay.

When we practice active leadership, we don't focus on the mundane. We don't focus on what's unimportant. We don't overcomplicate situations or concentrate on the drama. We do recall that there is a human being behind every issue. This human has specific needs and requirements that we, as their leader, should be able to provide at any time. We are aware of the perceptions our actions may create and we take responsibility for them. When we create a misperception, we see it, own up to what we've left behind, and immediately fix it. Our staff receives ad-hoc feedback in real-time. They know there are rules that they need to follow, which they do! They don't cut corners and get away with it—and it's not because big brother is watching—it's simply that they feel supported. They know their boss is passionate about wanting them to do the right thing. They are inspired, so they just do it. Our customers are also completely satisfied as a result. They only have to call once to get something they need since the employee is driven to do it right. The employee wants to do right by their manager who gives them the time that they need to feel valued, appreciated, aligned and supported. It's cyclical, and it's simple. Imagine a corporate culture that puts their staff first. Where the leaders work from their created leadership brand. Where they understand the needs and wants of their individual team members and provide it to them during each interaction. Where a unified continuum balances the distance between perceived narcissism and insecurity. Where there is a measurement of fluidity that all leaders understand will help them to maintain order—an internal order of true leadership, perceived as active and authentic.

THE
BASICS

ACTIVE LEADERSHIP

"Growing other leaders from the ranks isn't just the duty of the leader, it's an obligation."
— Warren Bennis

Three main components make up active leadership. First, effective feedback delivery. Second, self-awareness. And lastly, your leadership brand.

In its simplest form, active leadership is where the leader spends at least fifty percent of their time with their staff. This time could be spent coaching one-on-one, training, casually delivering feedback, in a formal review session, or discussing quality, future goals, any objections or any issues. Sometimes, it's just a check-in to see how they are feeling. If you're not focusing at least fifty percent of your time as a leader on your staff like this, they may perceive you as demonstrating shitty behaviour, or as being an inactive leader.

I know what some of you may be thinking. *How can I spend that much time with my staff when I have all the other work I have to do?* Yes, you're right, and it is a question worth asking. So, how *are* you going to do this? Assume from here on in that this is what is expected of you. You need to find a way to make it work. This is not tough love—it's reality. Leaders usually have a lot on their plates and have to use exceptional time management and organisational skills. You want to be less of a shitty leader, don't you? So, stop whining about time and keep reading.

Being an active leader is what drives change. It is what builds consistency, and it is what establishes the rules. Some employees will cut corners and take advantage where they can if they don't respect you as a leader, or the job. You have to teach them to care, and not to view this as just another job. How are you supposed to do this? By giving them an environment they care about. If your staff aren't in an environment they care about, they won't go above and beyond to meet the needs of a customer. They won't solve customers' problems, and that impacts the bottom line.

We are all customers of something, we all ring up call centres. You are reaching their customer service department anytime you have to call any company. The agent you reach is bound by guidelines, rules and metrics to be successful. Sometimes, however, companies overdo it. They regularly send misguided messages to their staff. "We want every call you do to be five minutes or less, but you have to achieve one hundred percent quality." So, is it quality or is it quantity? They leave their staff confused and frustrated. The agents wonder how they're supposed to deliver amazing quality, do everything they're supposed to, in five minutes or less. When you're actively leading, your staff should be happy to approach you with thoughts, raise concerns or just ask for guidance. The only way to get any closer to the best of both worlds is to give your team attention, to keep them encouraged, and to give them specific, constructive feedback. Perhaps you suggest that you and your employee listen to a call together. You might find their call control is good, but they could have changed something which would have reduced the time a little. Help them understand how to manage each interaction better, reducing their call time without compromising quality. Rather than leave them hanging in a state of flux, confused about quantity versus quality, you give your time to help them understand. This is a small but noticeable difference when you as the leader are being consistent, supportive and genuine.

Actively leading lets you get to the bottom line of how your staff perform, no matter what industry you're in. Sometimes, a non-work related conversation is just as important. This is where it can become grey for many companies. They don't want to get involved in anything non-work related, but that's where they make their mistake. Take an employee who is usually really engaging, happy, smiley with a great attitude. If one week I notice they're coming in sullen and withdrawn, then I need to find out what's going on. Now, I don't want to cross the line, get too personal or become a therapist. At the end of the day, I'm going to need to pull them aside and say, "Hey Samantha, is everything okay? You seem different, is there anything we can do? How can I help?"

INACTIVE LEADERSHIP

If you have an employee that is struggling and you do nothing about it, know that your silence is consent. You're potentially going to demotivate or uninspire a productive employee. If you are an inactive leader, then you may be demonstrating behaviours like mine when I started my first team manager job. I made it about me, and not about my staff; I was disengaging. I wouldn't link my one-on-ones and feedback together to establish a set course for the employee to develop, or to reveal, where they wanted to be. As an active leader, determine the baseline of every person that you support. By knowing that baseline, when they deviate from it, you can easily support them through these issues. You can gently help them correct course back to their baseline.

The culture that inactive leadership creates can range from demotivating to toxic. Shitty leaders give little to no feedback to staff, and any feedback that they do provide won't matter because the employees won't care. They just feel like a number. They don't feel like a person, they don't feel valued, and they don't feel aligned. Any feedback from a shitty leader is usually negative and without improvement recommendations. Staff will loathe coming into work. Attendance issues will be rife. Staff will be taking advantage of sick time, or they'll be looking for another job. Worse yet, they'll be sticking around, but they just won't care. Running a company based on active leadership means you will have employees that come into work because they want to. They will enjoy what they do and feel supported. In some of my consultative interviews, employees felt neglected for years. They never received feedback and some never even knew who their direct manager was. Years and years of no feedback—talk about silence being consent!

If you're demonstrating shitty leadership behaviours with minuscule self-awareness, then you're probably displaying traits that appear to make it all about you. Perhaps you are perceived as narcissistic or somewhat volatile. Your staff aren't too engaged, and they don't care about the job. They may even fear you. I have worked for shitty leaders who liked when their staff feared them. They thought this was a positive way to keep their team "on their toes". How long can you balance on your toes? Staff would show up, sure, but they probably don't have any interest in hearing what you have to say. Inactive leadership is a shitty situation for both the employee and the manager.

Shitty leaders generally hire other shitty leaders, because incompetence breeds incompetence. If I am a shitty leader, I don't have a clue what being an active leader is about, or I choose to ignore it because it's all just a bit too "fluffy" for me. I'm not going to be looking for active leadership when I hire my direct team. If I am at the director level and I'm a shitty leader who doesn't know it, then I'm going to look to hire people like me. I'm egocentric, or narcissistic, or I just don't care—I want to hire someone and not have to think about it. I'm thinking, if the person I hire is like me then they must be good because I'm great at my job, right? Narcissism at its finest.

JANE THE INACTIVE (SHITTY) LEADER

A major company hired me to run their training team. On day one, I met with the director, Jane, and she gave me a few key areas of focus. Great, I thought, at last, Jane was a manager with some direction! Alas, although I had monthly one-on-ones scheduled with her, I was lucky if I was able to reschedule them, as most times they didn't happen at all. I rarely saw her, and when I did, you bet she wasn't engaged. There was no personal touch to my welcome or induction. I felt isolated without a clear path or direction of action many times. In meetings, Jane would become aggressive about things that weren't going her way. Jane would belittle her direct reports in front of others. She was seldom clear on strategy or direction.

On a good day, we were stuck in what we referred to as administrative hell. My peers and I would struggle to achieve the irrational deadlines Jane set, only to have her turn around and say, "No, this is shit! This isn't what I wanted." The hypocrisy continued. At times, some of us would attempt to challenge back, asking for some level of clarity or guidance. The results were always underwhelming. The typical response was, "You're a senior leader, you should know." Had I realised my mind-reading skills were so well-known, I'd certainly have gone into a different profession.

Jane was a data-driven, numbers-focused manager. She rarely demonstrated a sincere or authentic people focus. I believe her background was statistics-based, and it showed in her great ability to work with data. She was well-versed with how her organisation was performing from a data and financial perspective. She did, however, require constant reminders that there were people behind those metrics. When her staff would fail—or rather, do things Jane didn't like—she would get fired up and emotional. Her reaction to the slightest of inconvenience caused by an employee would be, "Get them out of this business!" Jane would also need reminders that you can't just fire people because you don't like them or they made a miniscule mistake.

Jane was consistently good at being an inactive leader. She was full of contradiction, had many misunderstandings, and a lack of engagement. There was a perceived lack of any sincerity when she would give you a compliment, most of us didn't buy it. Most things felt like it was just another tick in a box. We were senior leaders attempting to lead well, seeking examples being set. Sadly, most of the time, there was nothing worthy to emulate. Jane created a name for herself within the organisation as consistently demonstrating bully-like behaviour. It was our job as her senior team to defend her when our direct reports accused her of doing something shitty, but how could we, when we all also believed she was a shitty leader? It's challenging when you're *not* a shitty leader, but you report to a shitty leader that you have to defend. Oh, the politics of corporate life.

Upon personal reflection while writing this chapter, there were some moments, although rare, where Jane did emulate active leadership traits. Albeit great to witness, these were not consistent behaviours. Like a spot of sunshine on a continuously cloudy day, she showed rare moments of authentic behaviour where she appeared to take an interest in others. I can recall that during these rare weather breaks, I was so inspired to see her effort that there was nothing I wouldn't have done to help and support her. During these rare times, I wanted to raise her up and defend her across a sea of negativity. Then, in true and unfortunately consistent shitty leadership behaviour form, a frigid cold front from the north appeared and the shittiness resumed. The sunshine was gone. Those rare moments at least showed me that *anyone* is capable of becoming less of a shitty leader—you just have to recognise the shittiness and work to fix it. It's all about choice. It's all about recognising where you're choosing to be on the ego continuum.

Jane was the epitome of an inactive leader who focused on numbers rather than people. To this day, I doubt that she was ever truly aware of what she left behind. If she did have any level of self-awareness, she hid it well or simply didn't care. Self-awareness and your ability to own it at all levels is a critical foundational step in reducing your levels of shitty leadership. We will delve into this more in the coming chapters. If you were a Jane, reading this today, hearing about experiences from an employee many years ago, how would you like to have been remembered? What impacts have you left behind?

We will delve more into the components of active leadership throughout the book. Bespoke feedback delivery is essential for building trust and rapport with your staff. This will help them feel comfortable enough to acknowledge and improve the behaviours that you've asked them to. With leadership branding and self-awareness, these components are more internalised for you, the learner. When authentically engaged, you will be accountable for your thoughts, feelings, behaviours and emotions. This approach holds you to a higher standard, ensuring that when you're emitting the behavioural outputs of a shitty leader, you can catch and fix them. We have only scratched the surface on this topic.

ACTIVE LEADERSHIP
Reflection Questions

› How do you define active leadership?
› How much time do you spend actively leading your teams today?
› What reflections occurred during Jane the Inactive Leader?
› Reflect on the term self-awareness and begin your authentic journey into this area – just reflect for now.
› What are you going to start doing that will help your current or future team?

LEARN HOW TO INSPIRE

"Live as if you were to die tomorrow. Learn as if you were to live forever."
— Gandhi

THE OXFORD DICTIONARY TELLS US INSPIRATION IS *to be stimulated (or motivated) to do or feel something, especially to do something creative.* So in essence, inspiration leads to motivation. And motivation is vital to active leadership.

Realise and recognise that leadership isn't really about you. Congratulations on your first leadership role, you've finally made it. Guess what? It is no longer about you. Deciding whether you're willing to give up the limelight is the first step in learning how to inspire others. Reflect: how often do you put others first in non-business situations today?

Be willing to make it about everyone else. Show humility. Give people your time to ensure that they are performing in the best possible way for themselves and your business. This is how you will create inspirational moments with your staff. The more time you invest in practising inspirational leadership, the easier your job will become! Set that tone.

Do you know what personally inspires you? What inspires you to want to be better? Why are you on this path of self-discovery? You bought this book (or you received it from a friend with excellent taste). What motivated you to read this book in the first place? What motivated you to understand your shitty leadership traits better? Why do you think it's important to become more self-aware, if you do?

INSPIRED BY KARIM

In 2015, a man I had the pleasure of managing eighteen years ago sent me a testimonial for my website. I asked Karim to provide me with his thoughts on my leadership skills. I hadn't spoken to him in years, yet he returned the email quickly, indicating he'd be happy to write something.

Karim is an incredible guy. I was working for a large computer company in the early 2000's, looking after their contact centre. Call volumes were seasonal, so we hired people on contract. I hired Karim when he was sixteen years old. He knocked my socks off in the interview. Karim was the youngest employee hired and was my last man standing. He out-performed others four times his age. When I reflect, I still don't understand where his work ethic came from, especially at such a young age. He inspired me to stop pre-judging anyone based solely on their age. I was not expecting him to do so well in that interview as a sixteen-year-old.

Karim's story is an excellent example of inspiration in a management-employee relationship. Not only did I help and inspire him, but he also inspires me, even today! I hired him as a part-time contact centre agent all those years ago, and now he's a partner in an account management company in Canada. His career has progressed, and according to Karim's testimonial, I had an impact on him. I humbly share the following.

> "Mark really mastered effective communication in a professional setting, and in my opinion, really broke down the traditional barrier between manager and direct report. Delivering constructive feedback with a genuine intention of solving a problem, and helping someone develop is an incredibly difficult thing to do, but Mark made it look easy. He is very light-hearted, with a great sense of humour, but with stern and objective focus, when he needed to be, which as a result was in the best interest of the employee and company. If I could sum up what I learnt from him in one sentence, it would be, we win together, we learn together. I've taken this basic principle of leadership and leveraged it throughout my career, and it has been without a doubt one of the most contributing factors to the success I've had this far."

How rewarding is it that? Almost two decades later I had no idea that I had made that impact on him. The humility and joy in reading his testimonial and seeing where he had driven his career was grounding. It is these stories that everyone should have the opportunity to receive. It is these rewards that I humbly and sincerely share with you. I've been honoured to help others just like Karim over my career by simply taking an interest in being an active leader. What he describes is merely me actively leading a team, nothing more. Think about the impact you can have on your employees' lives if you are willing to learn how to lead actively. I was, and still am, extremely humbled by his words.

Karim helped me recognise that age should never be a sole determining factor. I often wondered, "Who was this young kid?" Karim was so receptive and had the work ethic you'd expect of someone much older. We would hire the contractors in August, and keep them until January due to the seasonality of the back-to-school order rush. Even when work was limited, we retained Karim simply because we didn't want to lose him or his great work ethic. He made a lasting impression on us all.

INSPIRATION FROM TWO QUESTIONS

Active leadership, when properly executed, will create inspirational moments. It's those moments that you remember for a lifetime. Inspiring your staff as a leader doesn't come from cute posters with cliché quotes on cubicle walls. You're trying to approach managing your team from a non-cookie-cutter perspective. When you bake cookies, you use a cookie cutter so that the cookies turn out the same size. You're shoving beautifully individual bits of cookie dough into a mould which churns out identical cookies, and that's not inspiring. It's tasty and appealing, it's consistent, which may work well for cookies, but not for people and how they require support and feedback.

In well executed active leadership, there is nothing cookie-cutter about it. Sure, there are some fundamentals about leadership that are the same across the board. However, the approach you take with each person must be unique because you're talking about different people. Treat individuals as individuals. Learn how to deliver feedback specifically based on the receiver. Being an inspiring leader starts with getting to know your staff.

Whenever I start supporting a new team or a new team member, I always ask them two questions:

1. How do you like to be led?
2. How do you like to receive feedback?

Most times, the reaction I get is that they've never been asked that before.

In one of my consulting roles, part of my initial remit was to meet the staff. I met with the eleven staff in one-on-ones during my first week, and those were the first two questions I asked. Each one of them told me they'd never been asked that before, and they struggled to answer. After a great deal of prompting and asking leading questions, I eventually got a response to how they'd like me to lead them. For example, "Well, you know, I kind of like autonomy, I don't like to be micro-managed." I'd reply, "Good, I'd rather you did your job, and I did mine!" I'll sometimes make a joke and say, "Well, you know, actually I'm going to micro-manage you a lot... Until you show me that I don't have to." This way, we turn the banter into a bit of a challenge, with some humour.

It is not our role as leaders to perform the functions of our staff. That's not what actively leading is about. Let say, I have had an employee for five years, and let's assume they know how to do their job, and they know how to do it well. If there are any parts of their job they don't understand or that they don't like, we can discuss to see if we can improve on it. Maybe there's a way to do things differently. I ask for their opinion on what they would like to change within the organisation so we can improve things. Then I'll say to them, "What I hear about how you'd like me to lead you, is that you don't want to be micro-managed. Now how would you like to receive feedback?" I'd get back, "Oh, I've never been asked that either."

This becomes a dialogue; it's not clinical. After these first few questions, I know now that Joseph is very personable, very confident, and good at what he does. He is looking to progress in the future, and that's great! I can make a note that he wants to move up so I can start thinking in our future one-on-ones if he can do that. I'll make a mental note to find out what his motivation is for wanting to move up. I also know that from a feedback perspective, he is quite confident in his ability. If he makes a mistake, he wants to know about it right away.

In fact, he'll probably know about it before I do. He's proactive, so I know he will come to me about any mistake. I set the stage and say, "Listen, Joseph, if you ever do make a mistake and you think it might be detrimental, just come tell me about it right away. We'll fix it together." He'll say, "Mark, that's awesome, thank you for that. I appreciate that." He leaves our chat feeling motivated and inspired that his new manager is going to set him up for success. He knows if he has a significant shitty moment he can own it and we can fix it together. He's probably going to go and fix any mistake on his own; he'll come back to me and tell me when he's already finished correcting it. This is a by-product of non-shitty leadership starting to create positive outputs.

Whereas, I know that *Michael* is not as confident as Joseph. He needs a bit more validating and more support. I know that from some of the words he uses and from his feedback. Michael seemed more nervous than Joseph, more reserved. What I learnt about Michael is that he is very soft-spoken. He doesn't like conflict or arguing, and he keeps to himself at lunch. He comes to work ten minutes early and leaves on the clock every day. He is a steady Eddy and a loyal employee. He will be in this role until he retires. He has no interest in moving up. He has no interest in doing anything different. He just wants to come to work, do a good job, go home and leave work behind.

With Michael, I would have to approach feedback very differently. If I go too deep and too strong, Michael will close down and go internal. With Joseph, I can say, "Hey, help me understand what happened here because clearly, this wasn't right. What are you going to do differently next time? What are you doing, man, come on!" I don't have to be syrupy sweet with Joseph. If I were, he would get bored and would tell me to get to the point, that I was wasting his time.

I can't be that direct with Michael because he would get emotional. Instead, I'd say, "Michael, I noticed some areas in your statistics that I could help you with, I'd be happy to provide some feedback for you. I'd like to spend a few minutes talking about it with you so that I can point it out if you're not aware. We can figure out together how we can make sure that this improves moving forward. Are you open to that today?"

Because I'm not coming on too strong, Michael would get it. He'd be open to the feedback I want to give him. He won't feel like I'm attacking or judging him.

The result is that both employees leave motivated because they each received what they required. That is active leadership in motion. Take the time to ask your staff how they'd like to be motivated, to be led, and to receive feedback. It allows you to effectively plan how to actively lead them at an individual level. This starts you on your journey towards being less of a shitty leader.

LEARN HOW TO INSPIRE
Reflection Questions

› How much preparation time do you take before your employee meetings? Why?

› Pick three direct employees and in your next feedback sessions, ask them the two key questions from Page 30. Note their responses and start planning what you will immediately change moving forward.

› What was the initial reaction from your staff when you asked, "How do you like to receive feedback?"

HOW TO DELIVER FEEDBACK BASED ON THE RECEIVER

"What is the shortest word in the English language that contains the letters: abcdef? Answer: feedback. Don't forget that feedback is one of the essential elements of good communication."
— *Anonymous*

ONCE YOU ACCEPT A LEADERSHIP ROLE, YOU'LL need to understand what it means, authentically. If your focus is skewed and you continue to engage in behaviours that are perceived as making it all about you, you will be ineffective. No changes will occur.

Demonstrating a level of care and compassion is how you can address the needs of your staff. The perception of bossing people around won't gain you leadership points. You're likely to be perceived as egocentric, mean, or simply not a very effective leader. When you're asked about leadership, you say, "Oh, I get to tell people what to do, and I get to hire and fire." That's the sound of shitty leadership. I believe we manage the process and lead people. When you manage people, instead of the process, it becomes invasive. Most people prefer not to feel controlled.

As leaders, how do we lead those who don't particularly like feeling managed?

All you're doing when you're helping your employees develop in the ways that they want to grow, when you're challenging the ones that want to be challenged, is giving people what they've asked for. We're talking about the human dynamic of how people operate. When you have a conversation with new staff, you say, "Hi, it's really nice to meet you. I'm your new leader. I want us to make this a partnership. I want us to work together. I'm going to ask you some questions. I'd really like to know how you'd like to be led so that I can lead you in that way. You know, as a leader it's my job to give you feedback, both positive and constructive. Let's figure out the best way to do that for both of us so that you always have what you need, so you can feel motivated and inspired every day. How does that sound?"

Imagine going into your job with your new boss, and that is the conversation you have on day one. I am not recommending you regurgitate a script from a book. The concept is that you choose your own words to make it sincere and authentic. Most people would be surprised to hear this level of engagement from their leader. That has certainly been the common theme amongst my own personal experiences. In reality, it should simply be a dialogue between two people; aren't effective coaching sessions supposed to be just that?

So, if we know that staff would respond well to this level of engagement, why don't all leaders do it? Why don't managers have those in-your-face honest discussions with their employees about recognising what their role is, and take it seriously? Why aren't leaders saying that they're there to help their staff become better at what they do? That, if their direct reports fall, the leaders will catch them before they hit the floor? Isn't that what this is all about? If leadership to you is about ticking-a-box-because-I-have-to, you might need to dig a bit deeper and reflect on what matters, and how behavioural changes are led.

JOHN'S TESTIMONIAL - KEEPING IT REAL

John, who I worked with in a call centre, wrote:

> "Mark shares his gift of seeing opportunity in adversity, by focusing on simple, honest truths that build confidence. He draws on his own considerable experience to show you how obstacles can be overcome, while respecting the individual's need to forge a personalised plan for success. Open, personable and wise, I cannot imagine anyone who would not benefit from Mark's services."

John is talking about the benefits of authentic conversations. We're not defined by our failures but by how we choose to handle the feedback from those failures so that we learn and stop the cycle.

People who are new in their leadership roles can become overwhelmed when they aren't sure what they're supposed to be doing. They get emotional when things aren't going quite right or according to plan, so they resort to creating fear. One of the by-products of shitty leadership is invoking a fear culture. Once fear is the cornerstone of your environment, it is very hard for the employees to ever trust management again. For them, all leaders are lumped into one shitty pile.

A major component of actively leading is motivation, which is why you should engage in what you do—all of you—whether in the workplace or socially. The rationale behind what motivates a person is as vast as there are people on the planet. Most people are motivated by multiple things. Motivated to find out more? Read on!

According to Bob Kelleher at Dummies.com under their employee engagement section, "Extrinsic versus Intrinsic Motivation among Employees," there are two types of motivation.

EXTRINSIC MOTIVATION

"Extrinsic motivation comes from outside a person. For employees, the most obvious form of extrinsic motivation is money. Every paid job on this planet involves extrinsic motivation, whether in the shape of a salary, tips, commission, benefits, stock options, bribes, table scraps, or some combination thereof. Another example of extrinsic motivation is the threat of punishment. For example, an employee who regularly shows up late will be fired; so, fear of being fired may serve as an extrinsic motivation. Companies often use extrinsic motivation to encourage specific behaviours, such as competitiveness or punctuality. When people talk about engaged employees having both their heads and their hearts in their jobs, extrinsic motivation is the "head" part of that equation."

INTRINSIC MOTIVATION

"Intrinsic (internal) motivation: Intrinsic motivation comes from within. It's driven by personal interest or enjoyment in the task itself. For example, suppose you enjoy playing the pan flute, and you want to improve your skills. That's a case of intrinsic motivation. You don't want to become a better pan-flute player so you can be a world-famous musician – you simply want, for your own personal reasons, to improve your pan-flute skills because you enjoy playing the pan flute. With intrinsic motivation, the result is often growth – for example, growth as an intellectual journey or growth due to challenges that have been overcome. When people talk about engaged employees having both their heads and their hearts in their jobs, intrinsic motivation is the "heart" part of that equation."

In leadership, when we are looking at our staff, what do we know about their extrinsic and intrinsic goals? Do we understand what works for them? In many companies, there are reward schemes. The rewards are unsurprisingly cookie-cutter; a contact centre may offer £25 for 100% quality scores, or some derivative of that. As a leader, have you ever asked your employees if they cared about that £25 gift card? This approach is often repeated at a higher level when a manager tries to dangle the carrot of a promotion in front of an employee, "Listen, if you continue on this path and you do really well on *this*, and you do this, that and the other, then six months from now we might be looking at a promotion!" What if this particular employee simply doesn't want to be promoted or their personal lives don't require or support that change. What if they just don't care about being promoted. It might not matter to them, but you'll never know because you didn't ask. Remember, as a leader, it's okay to ask your employees what they want, need and sometimes, even feel.

Find out what motivates your employees at the heart level, look at all factors, and then incorporate these into your incentive plan and culture. If eighty percent of your staff are not motivated by money, then why do you have financial incentives? Isn't that defeating the purpose of a reward? It seems like common sense, but if common sense were really common, wouldn't everybody be doing it?

I was coaching an employee at a large computer company, and it was in the early stages of our relationship. In one of our first feedback sessions, some constructive elements needed to be discussed. I already knew how she liked to receive her feedback and how she liked to be led. I gave her the feedback, and she said, "Wait a minute, hold on! You're trying to change me as a person, and I'm not changing my personality for you!" I had to remind her that while I appreciated where she was coming from, she needed to recognise there was a difference between personality and behaviour. I acknowledged that she felt comfortable enough to challenge me. When employees question back, they're displaying an element of trust; this is progress.

Personality is who you are, and behaviour is what you do. We hired her due to the great person that she is—her personality is why she worked there. Under no circumstances whatsoever was I trying to change who she was as a person. What I was sharing was feedback regarding her *behavioural* choices, where behaviour is a by-product of her actions. It's what we do, it's not who we are. I was merely trying to point out the behaviours in real time that were counter-productive to her success. I wanted to help improve them together with her. It took her a while, as it can for some—the distinction can be confusing. With perseverance and persistence, she eventually saw the differences and her behaviours vastly improved.

It did make a world of difference for her in the end. She would talk about the fact that her role required her to work with a large number of people from different departments, in various countries. She struggled with how to effectively convince a diverse group that what she was working on was important, and how it could be beneficial for them. Through patient coaching, we helped build the confidence and tools that she still uses today. She commented on how supportive, positive and non-judgmental the approach was, and how it helped guide her to find realistic solutions that worked for her.

KEEPING IT ALIGNED

In my first shitty leadership example from the introduction, part of my self-discovery was when I recognised my team manager peers linking their one-on-ones with their staff members progressively. Every two weeks they would recall their conversations and action items through productive discussion in a manner that worked for the individual employee. There was nothing formulaic or cookie-cutter, just a dialogue about what they had previously discussed, and how it related to their outputs during the past two weeks. What had they done differently? What had they learned? How were they feeling? Had anything changed since the last session? What ad-hoc feedback had you as the leader provided. What had you seen and noticed?

If we circle back to the beginning, the entire concept of being an active, non-shitty leader is to help promote and influence the right behavioural changes within your staff. By documenting their progression, you drive the engagement to a new level. This not only demonstrates a supportive approach, but it also shows genuine caring for their well-being. It puts you on your first stage of becoming less of a shitty leader. How? By reducing some possible past misperceptions as you develop your self-awareness and leadership branding. Dare we say your humility is showing, and we think it looks great on you!

THE
PEOPLE
AND
THEIR
FEELINGS

HOW TO LEAD INDIVIDUALS INDIVIDUALLY

"No matter how good you think you are as a leader, my goodness, the people around you will have all kinds of ideas for how you can get better. So for me, the most fundamental thing about leadership is to have the humility to continue to get feedback and to try to get better – because your job is to try to help everybody else get better."
– Jim Yong Kim

GENERALLY, THE FIRST LEVEL OF LEADERSHIP IS the team manager role, sometimes also known as the team leader. This position should be responsible for delivering feedback and coaching to the front-line—the people that work directly with your customers. In other industries, these roles are often called the "supervisor," "assistant manager" or "manager." Team leaders can also perform other duties, but their primary function as a direct supporter of people should be to actively lead. These roles are generally entry-level management, where their manager manages other managers, and the journey upward continues. As you move up the management ladder where you're managing other managers instead of front-line employees, how does the non-shitty leadership demand change?

As you progress up the hierarchy, the active leadership demonstrated should be more relevant. In actuality, it's usually less. Team managers should be spending a minimum of fifty percent of their time actively leading and avoiding cookie-cutter leadership. As a reminder, cookie-cutter leadership is treating everybody the same in every job, without having any differentiation or nuance in how you approach your staff. This includes how you motivate, mentor, provide feedback, or lead. It can sound and feel robotic.

There's only so far that you can go when relying only on rudimentary feedback and leadership. If you want to help people perform better and make lasting behavioural changes, then there has to be a more active leadership approach.

This basic type of leadership may get you by, but it certainly won't progress your career nor will it lead to behavioural or cultural improvements. Some companies make do with the cookie-cutter approach, but there's usually no culture of feedback, and therefore no improvements. You have to decide where you want to be in your industry. If you want to be world-class, if you want to be known for service excellence within your industry, cookie-cutter, pardon the expression, won't cut it!

In the service industry today, the average consumer is a lot smarter. There are many social channels to contact a customer; it's not just simply over the phone anymore. There is live web chat, texting, email and social media. There are so many other avenues through which a consumer can contact you, so you need to be engaged to handle anything. Moreover, when the initial contact fails, the recovery to win back the customer is even tougher. Most of the time we won't get a second chance to make a first impression. So, get it right the first time and knock their socks off with service. In a competitive world, service is often the only differentiator.

If you look at utility companies, Company A doesn't have better gas than Company B. Company A doesn't have better electricity either. You never hear, "Oh, their electricity is so much better," or "Your water is better than mine."

The products of these companies are commodities. Their product never changes, so that's not a factor when it comes to business choice. Take mobile phone companies. Cell phone carriers are pretty much all the same. Their prices may differ, and they might have different packages, bundles, tariffs, or coverage areas but it will always come down to service. If your service is not up to that customer's standard, why should they remain loyal?

An individual employee should be held accountable to do their job well, but in order to make sure that they are changing their behaviour to do that, they need something better than cookie-cutter leadership. For the agents to be consistent in their approach, to offer superior service, excellence and a caring attitude to your customers, they need to be led actively. You can't teach people to care, but you can motivate them to have compassion, which will result in them inspiring themselves to care about their customer. Bottom line—employees who are treated right by their supervisors will pay that mantra forward to the customer. How would that improve your bottom line and culture?

EMPLOYEES ARE PEOPLE NOT NUMBERS

The most efficient way to prevent cookie-cutter leadership is to call it out when you see it. But what happens if you can't see it? You have to be able to recognise what cookie-cutter leadership looks and sounds like. An easy way to identify its occurrence is to look at your customers. The way you treat your employees will manifest in how your employees treat customers—and that's something you can directly measure. You can hear it in what your customers are saying, in your customer satisfaction scores and your level of complaints. You can see it in your emails and in your churn—your monthly input of new customers against how many customers left in that same time period. It's about understanding your business and being able to link things back to service. There's no greater source of insight than listening directly to what your customers say. Even your customers leaving without telling you why is very relevant.

My old boss Jane never demonstrated that employees are, in fact, people and not just numbers you control. But if you can remember that simple fact, then you have taken the foundational step towards active leadership and cookie-cutter avoidance. Recognising the individual as an individual, will instantly put you in the mind-set of knowing you can't treat Bill the same as you treat Jack. Bill and Jack are two different people. When you start recognising them as individuals, they no longer become employee one, two, three and employee four, five, and six. They're Jack and Bill, as they should be. What are Jack's needs and how do they differ from Bill's? What can I do to help support them better so that they recognise all the great skills they bring and the areas of development we can discover together?

What do you need to provide to help them develop and learn, so that both Jack *and* Bill can provide a world-class level of service to their customers each and every time? You can return to *Learn How to Inspire*, and ask them the two questions:

1. How do you like to be led?
2. How do you like to receive feedback?

That's where non-shitty leadership begins.

SELF - AWARENESS AS A LEADER

The Greek philosopher Socrates stated, "The unexamined life was not worth living." He also said, "True knowledge exists in knowing that you know nothing."

I have said for many years, "We don't know what we don't know". It's a fun statement you, almost like "Who's on First?" If you're not familiar with that classic Abbott & Costello skit, I'd recommend a web search.

> "When I don't know what I don't know, I don't know I don't know it. Then, if and when I take the time to know what I should know, I now know I don't know it, then I can learn to know it, so I know I know it, so now I know what I should know and I know that I know it and this makes me smarter to recognise there is a lot more I should know that I know I don't know. You know?"
>
> – Mark Robinson, 2017

To assess our abilities and behaviours, we need to scrutinise what goes on both internally and externally—what is commonly referred to as self-awareness.

We hear it all the time, in self-help books, in lectures, at work. How much do you actually know about what this means and how it links to becoming less of a shitty leader? Self-awareness can be further defined as the conscious knowledge of our character, feelings, motivations and desires.

Self-awareness is being cognizant of who you are, what you say, how you say it and of how what you have said is perceived by the individual receivers. Self-awareness is being mindful of what you leave behind when you walk away. It's being conscious of the impact that you are having on the people that you should be actively leading. Self-awareness is about knowing how you show up to different people. Do you sound condescending and patronising when you're supposed to be motivational and inspiring? What if you're giving feedback to an employee you don't personally like, can they feel and sense it? How do you lead people you don't personally like? How aware of self are you? If you're not very self-aware, perhaps you're demonstrating characteristics of shitty leadership.

To have a conversation—which in the realm of active leadership is often feedback—you and your staff member should be alone, in a comfortable environment.

Take this particular situation—I am providing you feedback. Am I self-aware enough to know that I don't sound like a shitty leader while delivering this feedback? Am I recognising who you are so that I am delivering your feedback in a way that is best for the you? Do you know that I'm actively leading? Do you understand that I am trying to tailor my approach to suit your needs? Do you need to know this?

The receiver—you, in the last example—also has a degree of accountability to choose acceptance over defensiveness, and to receive the feedback in the way it is intended—as a way of helping. Are you clear about your intent? Communication is all about intent. Why are you telling me this and why should I listen or care?

I remember one former manager providing me with feedback. She gave me three very positive components and one piece of constructive development. Upon hearing the positive, I sat there and smiled. I took it well since my insecurities back then, disguised as narcissism, knew how wonderful of an employee I was. When she delivered the constructive criticism, however, my glass house shattered. I chose to only focus on the one constructive piece. I became irrationally defensive and challenging, demonstrating some poor behavioural choices. The manager paused the feedback and highlighted what had just happened. I instantly recognised what I had done, what real-time choices I had made and thanked her for the insights. It was eye-opening to be able to recall the moment in time when I learned first-hand what self-awareness felt like. The irony is that sometimes, the feelings in these examples are only one-sided. I sent the mentor in this story a note years ago sharing and thanking her for what she helped me achieve. Her response was quite lacklustre and ultimately uninspiring; she seemed to not really care about the great impression she left with me. Although her lack of interest years later wasn't what I hoped, I chose to not let it negatively impact what she provided in the past. It just goes to show you that shitty leadership moments can happen at any time throughout our career. An event in time can have such a lasting impression on us, and not so much on the other party involved. That isn't always a reflection of shitty leadership, just an interesting point of irony.

SELF-AWARENESS IN THE WORKPLACE

In one of my leadership roles, I supported escalation complaint reps. This team assisted the office of the president of the company. These were very high-end level complaints. We had an available spot on our team, and I looked to hire externally for the role because I thought it would be good to bring in some outside talent to help us. We hadn't done this in more than a decade, so we felt it was a good steer. We ended up bringing on an employee who was a bit older than the average age of the team. Bringing in outside talent to a predominately longer-term internal team can help raise the bar.

I asked two of my team members to co-interview. It was a great opportunity to build their recruitment skills and make this a cohesive task. We interviewed and unanimously chose the same candidate. Within her first week, she had alienated about fifty percent of the team. Back then, new hires would shadow a team member to learn the job as part of their induction. This way, not only would she learn goodwill gestures and financial compensation elements, but also the systems and processes she'd need to understand for her to look up any complaining customer's account history. She was learning the job in real time.

As she was being trained, she continually cut who she was shadowing short, "Yeah, I know. Yeah, oh, I know that. I know that." All those she shadowed provided the same feedback. She learns very quickly and retains the knowledge well, but her tone and approach are very condescending, abrupt and sometimes rude.

She was commenting on procedures that were internal—there was no way that she could have known about them. Whether that was her insecurity manifesting or just words she was choosing to use, it was annoying her peers. She was frustrating them because they were always being interrupted, and her behaviours and actions were perceived as condescending and rude. It was not the peer perceptions one would hope after only a few days in the role.

As there were multiple pieces of feedback from a variety of different sources, I knew I had to act on it. Feedback delivery was required. I already knew that she was very direct; she didn't care much for the sugary sweet approach and just preferred her feedback direct and to the point. That is what she shared in her first one-on-one with me when I asked the two questions, so that is what I offered. The feedback was shared. She received it well without too much objection. I felt positive that perhaps things would change and we'd be able to move past these first few weeks of fear and insecurities common to some people. As time went on, however, the behaviours continued. Nothing changed, and the complaints about her continued. In fact, they intensified.

The complaints escalation team dealt with the finance team directly when processing customer refunds. I received a call from the finance manager advising that our new recruit was banned from ever engaging directly with the finance team because she was rude, obstinate, disrespectful, and very demanding. I joined a finance team meeting to better understand examples of these interactions. I spent an hour with the finance team listening to direct and specific feedback of what shadows she was leaving behind with this team.

She hadn't worked for us for very long, but again I had to pull her aside and provide feedback, "We need to discuss some comments I've received from the finance team about your interactions. This feedback is similar to the feedback previously provided in regards to communication with your own team."

The feedback was direct as she preferred and she listened. This time, she was completely surprised at the feedback from finance. She completely lacked any level of self-awareness in this area. She could accept our direct team feedback but struggled with this same feedback when it involved staff from outside our team. She insisted the finance team were simply insecure and didn't know how to engage someone as strong willed as she. She struggled with the notion that her behaviours and choice of tone and words were perceived as bullying. Even after providing recommendations on how to ask and engage an urgent work request—versus "do it now, and I'll wait"—she was unable to rationalise the difference in tone, attitude and behaviour.

We had now reached the stage where performance management was required. She had to make a choice—either work with us to fix these behaviours, or we'd have to part ways. It wasn't intended as a threat or an ultimatum, it had just reached the point where nothing was changing. My job as an active leader was to keep persisting, try different approaches, and then call her out directly and honestly when all else fails. I'm setting the expectations, and the staff need to recognise what those expectations are. It's my job to say, "We have been talking about the same thing for four months, and nothing's changed. Now I need your accountability, so I'm going to involve HR because it's not working. Either you don't know how to change it, you're not taking responsibility to change it, or you don't want to be here."

In this story, we involved HR, and nothing changed. We provided her with every opportunity, more so than I should have, and eventually, we terminated her employment. I was persistent on making an effort to try to get her to become self-aware, but you can't force someone to get there. The receiver of feedback, in this case, was not self-aware or willing enough to change her behaviour. I persevered, and when that failed, it got to the point where it had to be escalated. Even then I tried to bring her into the decision-making process. I tried to get her to recognise just how serious this was becoming because nothing was changing.

Obviously, I'm not going to keep coaching her in the same way. Nothing was changing. Coaching the individual as an individual means that sometimes, you have to try Plan B, Plan C and even Plan D. You have to try something different, and sometimes if the self-awareness is still not there by the receiver, you just have to be blatant and call it out. Sometimes you have to have a discussion about self-awareness. Ask your employee to tell you about their behaviour. Get them to help you understand how their actions are supportive and conducive to working as a successful team member. Ask those types of leading questions and then hopefully people start to recognise the impacts of their behaviour themselves. How are your staff affecting those around them and potentially their own career?

This employee honestly had no idea of the shadows she cast on her peers and the finance team. She truly believed she was just a strong individual. Even after many attempts at providing her with examples, having discussions with other managers and members of the finance team, she was unable to process her behavioural outputs as anything other than her simply being a strong-minded person. She believed the problem was the finance team's ability to work with her, and that she was just doing her job with the customers' best interests in mind. We agreed to disagree and moved on as sometimes you just have to. Not everyone can fit into your organisation.

Effective active leaders can set the stage for self-awareness development through a non-cookie cutter approach. Some receivers are not willing to be engaged, or they only want to be right, or they're just not ready to open that box and look inside. This is where performance management becomes your support structure. You can continue to provide direct feedback on what is happening with complete transparency so that there are no surprises. It is unfortunate when these situations occur, especially when we see them as avoidable. Remember, though, we are all different, and sometimes you will have an employee who is not ready to engage on the self-awareness journey. The end result may not be what you want, as was in the case above, but if they're not ready, you can't force someone's development.

The accountability and responsibility are theirs to receive, as well as the consequences based on the circumstances.

HOW TO LEAD INDIVIDUALS INDIVIDUALLY
Reflection Questions

› Make a list of your current staff and reflect on each of the following:

   a. What do you personally know about each one of them?

   b. Describe 3 positive and constructive behaviours from each of your staff. Don't share, this is just for you.

   c. Reflect on past employees and choose one who you personally didn't care for. Reflect on how you treated them and why. How do you think they personally felt about you?

› Reflect on a time when a former leader didn't give you the coaching you needed. Think about the situation and what resulted from the lack of support.

› What was the last shitty behaviour you demonstrated to a staff member? Upon reflection, why did you choose that one specifically and what made it shitty?

CATCH YOUR STAFF DOING THINGS RIGHT

"Leadership and learning are indispensable to each other."
– John Fitzgerald Kennedy

IN MANY COMPANIES, THERE IS A PREDISPOSITION to feedback being a negative experience. Upper management will always tell their staff when they are doing something wrong, but won't mention anything when they're doing things right. Feedback becomes this thing within each workplace culture, where staff think that they're only going to get called in to have a meeting when things have gone wrong. It can feel like a parent-child relationship at times. Why is that? When did feedback become the dreaded F-word?

That kind of mentality is not conducive to setting up your employees for success. You're not building trust. In fact, there's the possibility of creating an environment where everyone just feels demotivated and uninspired because it's always about the negative, it's always about what they could have done better, it's always about what they did wrong. When you, an employee, are always surrounded by that negativity, it may eventually take its toll. It's very hard to self-motivate when you're constantly on the verge of getting told that what you've done is wrong. It can make you feel that you just can't ever get anything right. When employees—and possibly the entire culture of an organisation—feels this way, how do we expect these same folks to go above and beyond for the customer?

If this negative environment is the norm, my experience is that staff will check out. They will stop caring, cut corners, and may not always do the right thing. They certainly won't be inspired to go above and beyond to satisfy the needs of their customers. They will call in sick when they're not, they will look for other jobs, and so, you may lose their skill that you hired them for in the first place. It's just not a fun environment to be in thirty-five to forty hours a week.

When you are not inspiring, your staff will not take creative risks. They will think they can't try something new because your staff is drowned in the fear that if their innovative idea doesn't work, they will be shamed, reprimanded, bullied or fired. Fear stifles creativity. Fear impedes the natural process of people wanting to do what's right.

Telling your staff that what they're doing is wrong all the time is a toxicity builder, so start catching them doing things right. It's okay to point out to them what needs improvement, but there should be a balance. Most importantly, the positive feedback should never be patronising or condescending; it should be sincere and genuine. Never talk to people like they're stupid while trying to make it look like you're genuine. "Now, we talked last week about your stats, and they're not getting any better. Do you know how to answer the phone? Do you want to go back in and have another feedback session? Let's go have another coaching session about the same thing that we've talked about for the last four weeks. Let's go do that now." That's not going to score you any points as a leader. In fact, this example is absolutely what shitty sounds like. Say it out loud in your most patronising voice. See how it feels.

Instead, be genuine and honest. When you hear someone make a good phone call say, "Listen, I just want to tell you, I walked by and heard you on the phone, that sounded great." To someone who's been struggling with their attendance, you might say, "I really noticed the effort you put in to arrive a few minutes early today, you know what? That's awesome. Keep it up." Even something as small as, "How was your weekend? Thanks for everything you did last week," can help relax the feedback atmosphere. Even a little effort goes a long way.

CATCHING THEM DOING THINGS RIGHT

If you have done your work in the previous chapters and have started to build a better rapport with your staff so that you understand how they like to be led and how they like to receive feedback, then catching them doing things right should be easy. You should know what motivates them, and you can pick which points to positively reinforce based on that knowledge. If you have an employee who is a little insecure, and they've been in that negative downer mode for years, and you know they're driven by positive feedback, try to help build them up. If you know that they've been struggling with a certain aspect of their call, focus on those calls. Do extra, quality side-by-sides. Any opportunity to spend more one-on-one time with your staff will always be well received.

Listen to what they're doing in their calls and use that as your motivator. "I hear and see a vast improvement in X area of this call. I see and hear it, and you know what, that is fantastic! You should feel really proud of yourself. Well done, keep it up. What do you need from me to ensure that you continue in this right direction? Because this is brilliant." Not rocket science, is it?

THE PERPETUAL CRIER

I had an employee who would burst into tears whenever she knew it was time for her one-on-ones, or even just that she had to come into my office. This started years before my arrival and was due to constant negativity leading to her repeatedly choosing to feel worthless.

She suffered from anxiety to begin with and was not always secure in herself. It was always very touch-and-go with her. As I became part of this team, I got to know her. I started doing my one-on-ones at her desk instead of having her come into my office, or we'd go for a walk. I didn't talk about anything personal. I started doing them more frequently so she'd get used to having a one-on-one dialogue with me. I wanted to build trust, be sensitive to her personal issues and not add any unnecessary stress to make her feel more anxious than she already did. She was a reliable worker, knew her stuff and only ever made the occasional error, as we all do at times.

Even when I didn't have anything constructive or remotely negative to say, she'd still get emotional. She'd completely miss what I was telling her because she was so caught up in her own fear of going into the manager's office. There was one instance where she solved a massive mess that would have cost the company thousands if the order had gone through incorrectly. I found out about her success so I called her in and said, "I'd really like to talk to you about something great." She looked at me warily, and I said, "It's all good, so relax." She came in. "I just wanted to say thank you. I just wanted to tell you that you did a fantastic job going over and above. You didn't have to go into that much detail, but you chose to because you felt something wasn't right. You researched, and you sorted it out. Well done, that was all I wanted to talk to you about."

Unfortunately, she got overwhelmed and started crying again—turns out we were damned if we did and damned if we didn't. It worked out well and eventually her anxiety did start subsiding around feedback issues. We actually spent an hour once talking about how she used to feel about past coaching sessions, which was the breakthrough she needed to articulate how she felt. She could own it. She stopped burying it, so it became a lot easier for the feedback to resonate well with her. She identified, through her own reflections, that not all leaders are shitty.

CONSTRUCTIVE FEEDBACK

For you as the leader, it's about creating a balance between saying positive things to your staff and not making things up. If you don't have anything constructive to say, then don't say anything. You don't have to do a one-on-one just to tick that box, just to say, "Well, I met with you because I need to meet with you twice a month to be an active leader, so therefore we met, but I've got nothing to say."

Instead, mix it up and ask, "So, what can I do more of? How can I better support you? What's something you've learned? What was something that was surprising? Do you have feedback for me as a leader? What should I do differently? Is there something I could do to better support you? What are your developmental goals for the future? Are you where you want to be?"

Obviously, don't ask all of these at once but there are options! In this way, you can still spend the time with your staff that being an active leader requires, without it getting stale, and without talking about the same basic stuff that you always talk about. Mix it up and have a real conversation. Learn something new about them.

Treat your employees like humans, it is not difficult. Take the opportunity to build more rapport. Elicit genuine feedback, and be receptive to their responses. If you're going to ask for it, you have to be open to receive it.

There are different levels of doing this, too. It doesn't always have to be an in-person meeting. Communicating with your employees can be a thank-you email, a card or a note left on their desk. It can just be a little treat. Bring doughnuts in for your staff, a fruit platter, or vegetables if you're that way inclined. It's about doing things above and beyond to say thank you in a genuine way, to say, "I'm here to catch you if you fall. My job is to build you up, not to shoot you down." That's how we build trust as leaders. That's how we become less shitty.

GENUINELY CARE

When I first started as a leader, I would make notes about people. I would remember that Janet's boyfriend is Joe, and he was going for a big job interview, so two weeks later when I meet with Janet I could ask her, "Hey, how was Joe's interview?" The response I always got was, "You remembered that?" I didn't hide anything, told them that I wrote it down because I wanted to ask them about it. Whether you remember on your own or you write it down, it shows you care enough to take an active interest in your staff's lives. Extending the olive branch first is a good way to help build rapport and trust.

I genuinely care about my staff, and I always want them to feel that I am trying to build that rapport with them. That was early on in my career. Later on, these skills developed more naturally. People are very appreciative when we remember the personal things they share with you. When you take a sincere interest in people, you will usually receive the same interest back. If you don't feel like you are receiving your staff's interest, then you get to use your newfound self-awareness to figure out why.

This sort of genuine rapport building with your staff just makes the workplace more enjoyable for everybody—for both you and your employees. It comes back to the company culture. What you've just read about is the beginning stages of creating a feedback culture. When your business does not have a culture of feedback, you're in the dark; you're not an informed, aligned and motivated workforce. You're the inverse of that, and you can't expect your staff to go above and beyond to become a world-class customer group or world-class whatever your industry is. It just doesn't happen.

CATCH YOUR STAFF DOING THINGS RIGHT
Reflection Questions

› Pick 5 direct employees and over the course of a week, pull them each aside. When the time warrants, only provide one piece of positive feedback about a behaviour or an action that you noticed they've demonstrated in real-time.

  › Use some of your notes from previous feedback sessions where constructive actions were agreed upon to find linkages.

› Caution: don't make it up—they have to have done something tangible here—an effort must have been made. Note their behavioural actions and how they performed post-feedback. How did it feel for you?

› For your direct staff who become emotional during your feedback sessions, detail a plan that you can use to help them. How will you build this plan to ensure it works well for them?

› During your feedback planning, choose three staff to ask for updates on personal areas you've previously noted. Be sincere and note their reactions, tone and body language.

FEEDBACK IS NOT AN F-WORD

"Whatever words we utter should be chosen with care for people will hear them and be influenced by them for good or ill."
– Buddha

When you think of the word feedback as an "F-word," you're probably thinking of a particular choice F-word that's not appropriate to use in the workplace. If you're like most employees and managers who hate the word feedback, you dislike the term because of the expectations it imposes, and how it generally feels for both you who has to deliver, and those who have to receive it.

Most leaders I have worked with in my career don't like giving feedback; they avoid it. The concept of feedback delivery can create that four-letter F-word feeling. Feedback, as you've already read, can quickly become perceived as a negative, which can cause that four-letter F-word feeling in your employee's gut too. Being on the receiving end of a continuous toxic environment that is not a culture of active leadership can impact some people at a cellular level. Consistently facing toxicity can start to affect our health. When feedback delivery is not engaged to benefit the receiver, the ship has sailed, the boat has sunk—we have lost the opportunity to positively influence and change behaviours.

The four letter F-word may not be what you think—it's actually "fear." Unless, of course, you really know your staff, and 'have taken the time with them to do all the things you've read about so far. In that case, your F-word might be neither "fear'" nor the expletive. Your F-word might instead be "fun," because you'll feel confident, prepared, and your staff will feel the same.

If I know that Janet is sensitive, and she's going through a rough time, I'm going to provide her with a bit of a reprieve. There are a couple of things I need to make sure she understands because it's impacting the business. However, I'm not going to be an ass about it. I'm going to be soft in my approach because I know Janet needs that at this time. I'm also going to recognise what she's going through in her personal life, so she knows that I'm sensitive to that. I may even say to her, "There are a couple of things performance-wise we need to talk about, but I recognise you're going through some personal stuff. Is this an okay time or should we defer until tomorrow?"

At the very least, I'm letting her know that I care enough about her to let it go for one more day. Sometimes that's all you need to do. She will remember that and find the appreciation for it in the future. When she does, she will pay it forward to a colleague or customer, and that is the ultimate win-win.

Many times you will find that the empathy you showed was enough for them to say, "Actually, it's fine, I appreciate your sensitivity, I shouldn't let this affect my work life." You're coaching them back to business, and sometimes your staff needs that distraction. Following along with everything in this book will change the F-word to "fun," or at least it will reduce feedback to not be as severe as people think it is. When feedback is not an F-word, leaders will actually deliver it, and employees will openly receive it.

SILENCE IS CONSENT

Sometimes, when you say nothing, you say everything. Keith Whitley, Alison Krauss and Ronan Keating all knew what they were singing about with their song "You Say It Best When You Say Nothing at All." It has always stuck in my head. Imagine you're walking down the street when you see two people arguing and it turns violent. If you don't do anything about it, then you are condoning that behaviour by not getting involved. If you see someone getting abused and you don't help him or her then you're enabling the abuser to keep doing it. I recognise that people don't want to get involved with strangers, because sometimes when you do, it ends up not working out so well for the individual who was trying to help. These types of crossroads pose awkward points of discussion.

From a leadership and feedback perspective, when you see your staff doing things they shouldn't be, and you don't do anything about it, you're condoning that behaviour. You can't then turn around and tell them not to do it months later when they've been doing it all this time. Now you become a hypocrite. You will lose credibility. At first, it could appear as nit-picking; your employees might say, "Oh my God, are you telling me something I'm doing wrong, again?"

Think about how you approach the situation, how you recognise it and about how you will deliver the feedback. I've seen people shopping online while at work while fourteen calls were waiting in the queue. I know there's something wrong with the feedback behaviour at that company. That's not acceptable to me. If the management at the company were doing feedback right, then that simply wouldn't be happening because those agents would *care* that fourteen calls were waiting in the queue. In those types of places people might say, "Well, yeah. I'm shopping online because I'm on my lunch break."

Okay, I get that, but inversely, I've seen call centres whose agents see the build-up of calls waiting, and instead they say, "You know what, I'm not going to take my lunch right now as I had planned to. I'm going to defer my lunch for 20 minutes because I want to help resolve some of this queue noise."

It is entirely possible to create a workplace where your team will care enough to postpone their breaks to help the company, but employees won't do that in an environment where they're not treated well.

In one company I consulted for, the team managers were completely disengaged. They would walk by and say nothing when there was a bunch of agents not answering calls. This even went up a level to the senior management. I saw senior leaders walk by team managers on their mobile phones when *fifty* calls were waiting in the queue. The team managers were on their personal phones, not doing anything, and the senior leaders just walked by. What are you doing? What are you doing right now? There's so much that goes on in that contact centre, and the management didn't have the level of diligence that was needed to make sure it was running like a well-oiled machine. This was a silence-is-consent environment where no one said anything, so no one did anything.

This had become the norm for years, and the agents took full advantage of it. You can't really blame them for that. "You've never said anything about this, so how was I supposed to know it was a problem? I've been doing this for eight years."

We sometimes inadvertently, via shitty leadership, breed our own incompetence.

When you see a change in your staff, when you get a "thank you" for your feedback, coaching, or one-on-one session where you wouldn't normally—that's when you know as a leader that you are creating a great feedback culture. Things that were issues before will no longer be issues, and people will come together. There will be a feeling in the environment that things are changing. You see smiles on faces, less absenteeism, less customer noise, fewer complaints. That's how you know it's working; that's how you know you're starting to do things right. You'll feel less shitty yourself.

FEEDBACK IS NOT AN F-WORD
Reflection Questions

› Reflect on a time when you recognised your silence was consent. Ask yourself why you chose not to react or provide immediate feedback during that period, even when you knew you should have done something. What will you do differently now that you've become more self-aware of its importance?

› Describe an experience from a past leader when you felt you were properly coached. Why did this one stand out?

› Define some key reflections three months post your feedback delivery improvements and highlights. Submit your stories to mark@ego-continuum.co.uk and you may be featured on our website.

THE
FINE
PRINT

WHY YOUR STAFF QUIT

"To effectively communicate, we must realise that we are all different in the way we perceive the world and use this understanding as a guide to our communication with others."
– Tony Robbins

There was a survey, back in Canada, from the late eighties which polled employees as to why they quit their jobs. The study found that eighty-six percent quit their job in the last three years because of their direct manager. On a more recent note, in 2014, Forbes claimed that sixty-four percent of employees leave their boss rather than the job. So, what does this mean and why should we care? If we actively lead and follow a plan that helps us become more aware of who we are as leaders, then we can proactively avoid our staff quitting and leaving because of us. Now, if they want to leave for reasons other than how their manager treats them, then we can't control those outside influences. We do, however, have the power to reduce attrition, because of our behaviours.

If staff are leaving because of personal reasons, because they don't like commuting, they have a better job offer, they are offered better benefits elsewhere, or because they don't like the company, that's a different discussion. The fact remains that 64–86 percent is too high a number to be leaving because of a shitty manager. When I talk to people about leadership and share my ideas about what I do, everybody always has at least two or three people or companies they recommend I should go visit. "Man, I wish you knew this person." Or, "We really need you in our company." Or, "I need to hire you to do this." It's amazing—and sad—how many people can resonate with the concept of shitty leadership. These were the same feelings I experienced when finalising the tagline for this book.

THOSE WHO QUIT AND STAY

If you have a team of people who have quit but haven't left, your team's productivity is at risk. The risk of errors and rework will be higher; your attrition rates may increase if your staff are seeking roles in other areas of the company. The outputs may show that you have a team of low-performing, under-motivated people, who are not aligned, not engaged, and not demonstrating that they care. It may manifest itself in your workplace culture. The leader must recognise that people are quitting but staying. They need to have the courage to better understand why, and that they might be the cause. Otherwise, the cycle will just perpetuate, and things won't change.

I was consulting for a company, helping them with their training. When I arrived, the leaders were disengaged. There was minimal feedback shared with a culture that at times, felt like blame and shame. The lack of support was corporate-wide. Leaders would avoid providing feedback, they gave very little direction and did not treat their employees as individuals. These behaviours perpetuated a culture of apathy from many of the employees I came in contact with. They wanted to care and some did. These workers were hopeful and believed that change was possible. Unfortunately, in true shitty leadership fashion, the iron fist would come down like clockwork, and any ray of hope would again diminish. When times became busy, or results weren't stellar, the yelling, cookie cutter approach was used for everyone. They would pull training, coaching and feedback and replace it with "Go, go, go. Sell, sell, sell. Do, do, do."

Middle management was stuck between a rock and a hard place. They were corporately inclined to support their boss, to do what he or she said—but they also wanted to support their staff, because, at the end of the day, they're the ones that served the customers.

If you, as an employee, are constantly barraged with shitty leadership and ineffective support, there will come a time when you throw in the towel. Maybe you're well paid, though, or maybe you get unlimited sick days, or maybe you know that HR doesn't follow through, so you're not going to get feedback anyway. You could be in a job for six years, performing below expectations through that entire time, and you still would have your job. Why *wouldn't* you stick it out? You start taking longer lunches; you go for more frequent smoke breaks. When you don't care, you don't follow through with the customer complaints, you don't follow through with the issues, you don't even do the basics because no one gives you the impression that they care, so why should you?

I can humbly say, there haven't been many times that I have had to terminate someone when they didn't know it was coming. I've always tried to be very open and transparent, as we should be. When actively leading is in good motion, we're following a process, we're documenting everything. If we've gone through a formal process, which is usually supported by human resources, then due diligence for all involved has been followed. You've tried coaching, you've tried feedback, you've tried giving support, you've mixed it up, you've asked them and said it all. If they're still not where they need to be, a decision just needs to be made.

As the leader, you've taken accountability, but there comes a time when you have to draw that line. You have to create a demarcation point that says, "I'm no longer accountable for this because I've done everything that I can do. I've used all my tips and tricks, I've pulled everything from my hat, and you're not responding. It appears that you're choosing not to change the behaviours we've talked about, as they're still counterproductive to the team, to your performance and our customers, so we have to go formal. What that means is, I will now get HR involved and this will move to disciplinary action. In a certain amount of time, if things don't change, that could mean we terminate your employment. It's not a threat, it's a leader's responsibility to do that. We simply can't have you continue this behaviour because it's counterproductive to you, the team, to me, and the customer."

That style of conversation can even be the straw that breaks the camel's back, that finally makes them think, "Oh, maybe I really do need to step it up." Especially if there's a culture that has perpetuated shittiness for a very long time, they've probably never taken the discussion of being terminated seriously.

From there, when you go formal and you follow your company's process, HR will get involved. If you're communicating effectively, it usually will continue for maybe six to twelve weeks, depending on the performance improvement, and if it's a unionised environment. If it's a robust performance-management process, it shouldn't drag on for more than ninety days. You set the plan and show your employee the clear expectations of what you need them to accomplish in the next ninety days. Don't set any more than three goals, and make them very clear. I would have SMART goals, that are specific, measurable, attainable, realistic, and time-bound, and I would communicate that. I would create the plan with the employee while they are as engaged as they can be, so that they understand the buy-in and the agreement. Then, I would move the coaching to weekly instead of fortnightly.

By week three, if nothing has changed, I would call another disciplinary meeting with HR where I would just say, "We're getting to the point now where we're meeting weekly and the changes are not showing as we've discussed. We decided what "good" looks like, and you're nowhere near that at this point. We all have invested a lot of time and effort into this, and your level of improvement is not matching. Can you help me understand what you're going to do differently and what I'm going to see next week? I need to start seeing some ownership from you on this because right now, I feel the ownership is on me. Do you want this to change? Do you want to work here? Do you want to go somewhere else? What are the reasons behind your choosing not to change? Because that is not an option anymore."

If you're clear and respectful, still delivering the feedback in a way that works for them, then that's great. However, when it reaches that point, there's nothing wrong in showing your employees that you're frustrated with them. Frustration doesn't have to impact respect. Always remember you are trying to help them uncover the reasons behind why things are not changing.

As long as they recognise that it's not personal. "I'm not citing you as a bad person, I'm citing that you're choosing not to make the changes that you need to, to be successful in your job. That's a decision that you are choosing to make."

A CHANGE OF CULTURE

The only way that you can change a quitting-and-staying culture is to start from the top down. Unless you get the buy-in from your senior leaders who influence change, who understand it's not just ticking a box or lip service, who actually want to drive change, nothing will happen. If you start people on a re-energising commitment, you can actually make a difference within three months. I've seen it. It all stems from the top down, every time. It takes a commitment and a behavioural change because you have to build the trust back, and you have to be consistent. You have to follow through, and realise that there is going to be an investment in doing this, but the payoff is so great. It should be a no-brainer.

The majority of the companies I work with have been very data-driven. There is always a commitment to the arms of business, whether it's technical support, customer service, complaints, sales, to drive change, to increase profit or to reduce cost. That is a given. We all know and understand how business works, but that's not the scope of this book. This is about people, leadership and the influences that leadership has on your staff and the overall culture. The people I have seen demonstrate shitty leadership from their behaviours were not well grounded in their people skills. They were very data-driven, and they enforced that data-drive down their leadership chain, all the way onto their staff. Data was first, people second.

If average handle time is too high, you need to bring it down. That compromises quality, so am I supposed to give good service or am I supposed to follow the quality prompts? How do you tell an agent who is clocking an average handle time of 550 seconds that you need their calls to be under 400 seconds, but they need to provide first-call resolution and fix everything, be pleasant and follow all of the governance that they've been taught? It is quality versus quantity. At the end of the day, in business, there is a constant barrage of contradiction. When senior leaders want to improve their bottom-line—which ultimately impacts their bonus—they hit up their front-line and say, "Well, speed it up. Stop the coaching. Get everyone on the phones, and do this, this, and this."

What that does is it takes away the people's support. The staff are being told that they're making careless mistakes, they are being called out and being held accountable for those errors, but the leaders are not looking at the ad-hoc behaviours in real-time that will drive the change. The senior leaders pull that ad-hoc feedback because they think it impacts cost, which is what they are motivated by, but it actually adds to the cost because the agents who do the work are not getting their required support.

It becomes this cycle of shittiness. Whereas, if you just let the leaders support the frontline well through feedback, behavioural counselling and coaching, you would create an aligned and motivated workforce. Your staff would automatically want to do the right thing because they feel believed in, they feel valued, and they feel supported. They know their manager or leader has their back. When you create a culture of support, people generally want to pay it forward, and it's usually to the customer.

WHY YOUR STAFF QUIT
Reflection Questions

› Reflect on a time when you quit a job but stayed. How did you feel? Why did you stay?

› Reflect on a time when you may have worked for a boss who quit and stayed. What was it like to work for someone who demonstrated those behaviours? How did that make you feel as an employee?

› Describe some of the challenges of coaching staff members who quit yet stay versus those who want to remain.

HOW TO BUILD YOUR LEADERSHIP BRAND

"Your personal brand is what people say about you when you are not in the room – remember that. And more importantly, let's discover why!"
– Chris Ducker

What is your leadership brand? Are you a shitty leader? Your leadership brand is how you want to be known, seen and perceived as a leader. Answer the following for yourself:

› Do you know how your staff and peers perceive certain behaviours you demonstrate?
› Have you ever felt like you were sometimes misunderstood as a leader?
› What is your current leadership brand?
› Have you ever solicited feedback from other people regarding how you're perceived as a leader?
› How willing are you to travel down this road of discovery?
› What will happen if you don't like what you find?
› Do some see you as a shitty leader? If so, why?
› How do you know what aspects of your leadership skill set you need to improve?

› Do you have the ability to honestly look inside and call out your own shitty behaviours?
› How do you know you're giving your staff what they need unless you've asked them, or have gotten them to give you honest feedback?

When you don't have a solid understanding of your own brand, then how will others know how to perceive you? Fear can become your brand if you don't take the time to build relationships. If fear were your brand, many would not want to work with or for you. If you're the type of leader that is intimidating, and no one's ever had the courage to provide you with direct feedback, or if no one can trust that you can professionally handle hearing their truth, then odds are, your self-awareness may be quite low in this area.

Most people don't ever think about their leadership brand. They don't know such a thing exists. They have never thought about how they're perceived as a leader. It can be a very eye-opening concept to think about, the natural by-product of which is that you can't help but become self-aware. Thinking about your leadership brand just creates that thought process—you can't un-think it once you know about it. This is commonly referred to as a form of Perception Management.

HOW TO BUILD YOUR LEADERSHIP BRAND

To build what your own leadership brand is, the first step is doing a self-awareness checklist. What do you think your leadership brand is? How do you think people perceive you? How do you think you deliver feedback? How do these reflect on your own personal values?

It's not all about being liked. There's a likability factor, but it's usually what you do and how you do it that makes people like you or not. Being liked should not be a priority. You want to be respected. You want to be valued. You want to be trusted. You want to be seen as a credible leader. Being liked is a part of that, but it should not be the primary motivator.

It's also okay to be feared a little, there's nothing wrong with that as we have discussed before. It doesn't motivate most people, maybe a small handful at best, but you *can* use it as a catalyst. When you actively lead and you're engaged and happy, becoming tough and showing strength, courage or determination can sometimes be perceived as fear. It's temporary, only because it's not normally what you demonstrate. That's okay, as long as you continue to demonstrate your self-awareness and communicate effectively the intent of why you're showing this. You don't want fear to be your brand, it shouldn't be mainstream, only for your exceptions.

HOW YOU SHOULD BE SEEN AS A LEADER

As a leader, I want to be seen as fair and honest. I want to be respected because I give respect in return. Respect should be earned. I want to be seen as tough but fair, challenging, goal-setting, inspirational, motivational, direct, as someone who gives people what they need, has their back if they fall, delivers feedback in the right way, and encourages people.

I want my staff to know that showing vulnerability to me is not seen as failure or as weakness, but as strength. Having the courage to show vulnerability in my opinion shows a wealth of humanity, and shows that a person cares enough to want change by having the strength to declare that they require some form of assistance. These types of engagements are sometimes heartfelt, thought provoking or emotional releases. Personally, I wear my heart on my sleeve. Whether it's a Canadian thing or it is simply a sign of the person I have become, I am not afraid to show emotion. Showing emotion and being emotional are quite different. I don't fly off the handle and respond to situations emotionally, but I can show emotion when required. See the difference? See how some could misperceive these? I am also very passionate about most things. This passion manifests itself as excitement, where some in the past have perceived it as anger. I am not an angry person at all, in fact, I find most things funny—including things I probably shouldn't. It can be very easy to misperceive so as part of my own personal leadership brand I would state:

> I wear my heart on my sleeve; I am empathetic. I am sensitive to what other people are feeling. This makes me in tune with emotions—yours and mine—versus acting from an emotional place.
>
> I am passionate about most things; you will see and hear this when I talk fast and my tone changes – it's all about excitement, not anger or frustration.

Remember we discussed how communication is all about intent? Our intent is helping people understand whom we are as leaders through a better understanding of the way we show up. So in my case, when you see me respond to your sad news, I am not being condescending or belittling, I am feeling what you're feeling. When you improve a behaviour we've worked on for months and you've demonstrated great success, that passion you're seeing isn't anger—I am genuinely excited and thrilled for you because I know how hard you've worked and the results are showing. And, because I took the time to share with you who I am, and you took the time to listen and learn who I am, we have this connection that bypasses all unnecessary misperceptions so we can focus on the matters that truly help make a difference.

Another reflection, is the kind of a leader you have. If you're a leader, you report to a leader; what would you recognise as your leader's leadership brand? If your brand is different from theirs, sometimes that can cause conflict, especially if your current leader is a shitty one. If you're a leader who works for a shitty leader, and your brand is different from theirs—which it *should be*—they may comment that you're too emotional or that you discuss things too much. Some see things like this as a weakness. How do you avoid compromising your own brand to support a shitty leader?

There's a saying that perception is reality, and while I get that, I don't fully agree with it. Perception is reality in the eye of the perceiver. Someone could think that I'm egotistical because I'm confident and they are not, or they have fewer confident moments. When they come across as someone who's confident, they struggle or can't relate to it because they can't identify with it, so they assume conceit. They assume arrogance. Their perception of me is an egotist, which is not true, but the perception is reality for them. So it's reality for the perceiver, but it's not true reality. I want to help them not to see me as such because that's not who I am, and that's certainly not what my brand is, or how I want to be perceived. If I fight it, then they will think, "Why are you acting guilty? Why are you getting angry? Clearly I have hit a nerve."

It's not about me trying to prove them wrong, it's me helping to show them correct behaviour. Instead of me coming back to them and saying, "You're wrong. Don't think of me like that because I'm not like that," with my finger pointing in their face, I'd say, "Listen, thank you so much for this feedback. I might not necessarily agree with all of it but I really do appreciate it. I recognise how hard it would have been to say this, so let's sit down together and work out an action plan for me, so that I can start demonstrating the qualities that you need in me as a leader." Ultimately, two things may have occurred: I stepped outside my normal behaviour which was causing the misperceptions, which I now need to own and fix, or they are just not self-aware enough to see the reality of the situation.

Done. Choosing kindness and acceptance will always help you to demonstrate humility, build trust and character, and help others to become more self-aware each and every time.

THE SHADOWS THAT YOU CAST

Part of recognising your brand is learning how to become self-aware and understanding how you're perceived. The shadows that you cast can be found from feedback forms you provide. This is especially true if you have an honest crew or if you've done it confidentially, where the employees feel safe giving you honest feedback without fear of retaliation. You will instantly learn from their feedback what you leave behind. If you're a positive leader, if you're a fair leader, if you're great at delivering feedback, then you will leave behind that air of fairness and support. If you are a shitty leader, you will find you're leaving behind a path of fear, toxicity, frustration, apathy, and lack of caring. If this is the case, clearly you have some work to do.

If you don't engage in confidential feedback forms, there are many other options. As in your learnings about effective feedback delivery and asking your staff how they prefer to receive it, you can also just simply ask. Engage in your own vulnerability discussions and declare that you're trying to become more self-aware as a leader, so do they have any feedback for you? See how they respond.

You can also find some quiet time, and use reflection exercises to think back on past experiences. Reflect on those times when you can recall upsetting your staff, or times when you felt frustration, despair, or felt isolated at work. These heightened times can manifest what I like to call "our shitty moments" when we have no intent on being shitty leaders but our behaviour indicates otherwise. Regardless of the method you choose, be willing to look inside truthfully in order to understand how you can, once and for all, take back your control and truly inspire others through active non-shitty leadership.

Once you have the feedback and you recognise the shadows that you cast, then it's up to you to take accountability as the leader to un-shittify yourself by focusing on the true feedback. You may have to force yourself to look at that feedback as a gift, even though you may be tempted to retaliate or challenge it because you're choosing to see it as negative—this is where you really get to show your humility.

Take a deep breath, regardless of whether you agree with the feedback or not. Accept it for what it is—it may not be your truth, but assume it's theirs. Reflect on how difficult it must have been for them to write and share this. You will instantly earn the trust and admiration of the people that might not have felt that way about you before. You're becoming self-aware, while showing your staff that you are doing so, which in turn will allow you to manage their perceptions that you created in the first place.

Many years ago at a technology company, I had a team of about thirty-eight direct reports. I managed to conduct bi-weekly one-on-ones and enjoyed them immensely. My team and I had a great rapport and we all worked quite well together. The company conducted twice-yearly employee surveys where the employees took a confidential survey to share their thoughts, views and opinions. The survey also had a management section where the direct reports could answer questions about their manager in a completely confidential manner.

I received my results, and I scored nineteen percent favourable on the question "My manger is effective at managing people." I was shocked. I was hurt. I was alone in a hotel room, working far from home. I felt crushed and defeated. It felt like no-one on my team was ever honest with me. How could this happen? Back then, if I had been local to the office I may have made some immature comment, using humour as my disguise. In my hotel, on the other side of the country, I had a few glasses of wine and reflected, made a plan for my course of action to get even with each and every one of those traitors.

A few days later back in the office I called a meeting. The team knew the meeting was about the feedback provided. I can still remember the look of shame, the lack of eye contact, the smug smiles—all in my head of course—but nonetheless, that's how it felt. I took a deep breath and began the journey of change. None of the personal silliness mattered anymore because an issue had been identified and I was ready to take ownership. I publicly and sincerely thanked them for their honesty. I applauded their ability to provide me with their truth. I wanted them to know I took their collective feedback very seriously and was going to take full ownership of breaking this feedback down further to help me develop into the leader they deserved.

I asked our HR team to conduct a 360-feedback session without me, to capture in more detail some of the why's behind their feedback. Over six months the team worked to provide me with detailed feedback. I took complete ownership and I felt some very positive changes. Six months later, to my delight, the same question this time scored ninety-one percent favourable. The bulk of the commentary this time focused on how well they felt I received the feedback, showed humility and was willing and open to change. It was an amazing opportunity for me to step outside myself and to really look with my eyes wide open. What I saw, I didn't like, so I chose to change it and thanked them all for their belief that their honest feedback would be the catalyst for the changes I needed.

Sometimes self-awareness truly comes to light when we least expect it. I cherish these moments always!

HOW TO BUILD YOUR LEADERSHIP BRAND
Reflection Questions

› What personal values of yours affect the way that you work? What do you stand for?

› What are the top behaviours of your leadership brand? What do you display often? How would you explain this to your staff?

› What are some common misperceptions about you?

› Describe how you want others to feel when you engage in feedback delivery.

› Reflect on a time when you may have cast a shadow that you didn't mean to or want to cast. What did you leave behind?

› Reflect on a time when you perceived someone incorrectly. How did you realise the perception was incorrect? What did you do about it?

For more development opportunities in building up your leadership brand and to use our templates, visit our website at www.ego-continuum.co.uk

THE MOST MISSED LEADERSHIP BEHAVIOUR

"On the highest throne in the world, we still sit only on our own bottom."
– Michel de Montaigne, The Complete Essays

In my years of asking the question, "What is the most missed leadership quality?", it's rare that anyone actually matches my response. I hear trust, respect, honesty, guidance, or support. It's not that they're not important—they definitely are, but they're just not the *most* important in my personal opinion.

Humility. People rarely think of humility because many don't ever think about what humility actually means. People could argue this and say, "Well, I don't think humility is number one for me, but it's in my Top 10." It doesn't matter where it lands on your list at the moment. You know it's number one on mine so we can discover what that means together here.

Humility is the quality or condition of being humble, of modest opinion of one's own importance, according to Merriam Webster's dictionary. As we talked about earlier, the first thing I always tell new leaders is, "Welcome to leadership, it's no longer about you." I never want someone to come back to me and say, "I wish you had said that to me twenty years ago when I started in leadership." I want to be able to help revolutionise the way that leaders are trained from the beginning. When we get fresh leaders, using that opportunity to teach them about humility and the importance of it helps incorporate humility in their brand from day one. It stops them from learning shitty behaviours from other shitty leaders, because humility can't be faked. You're either humble or you're not. Some people think leaders are born and not made. I don't necessarily agree with that because it is possible to help change others who display shitty leadership behaviours into non-shitty leaders through coaching, support and self-awareness.

When I close my eyes and reflect on some past leaders who thought they were effective, but clearly were not, I can usually link their ineffectiveness back to humility. The reason why an attribute like respect is good, but doesn't sit in the top position of my list, is that respect can be faked. I don't care if my staff respect me—they should, but respect should be earned. I'd never force it from them. It's not that I don't care, but don't respect me because of a title; respect me for what I do with it. Respect me for the behaviours that I demonstrate. Effectively and consistently demonstrating those behaviours that are productive, that help un-shittify a leader, can always be linked back to humility. You can't fake humility. It's part of your leadership brand, it can link back to vulnerability and it can absolutely help you demonstrate non-shitty leadership behaviours. It also ties directly into The Ego Continuum.

THE MOST MISSED LEADERSHIP BEHAVIOUR
Reflection Questions

› What was your initial reaction when you read that humility is the number one leadership trait?

› Reflect on your past leaders: how many demonstrated humility? Where do they land on your top ten list of best leaders you've worked for and why? What else did they do that worked for you? Why did these traits work for you, and would they now?

THE IMPORTANCE OF HONESTY

"If you do not tell the truth about yourself you cannot tell it about other people."
– Virginia Woolf

Honesty is part of the effective feedback delivery journey, from an active leadership perspective. If you're not being honest in the feedback delivery and in performance management, then the behaviours won't change to have a lasting effect. There is, of course, a fine line though.

You have to understand the relationship you have with the employee. If you turn around and say, "You suck, you shouldn't be working here," then obviously, you're being shitty. Some leaders think honesty is just being direct and blurting out whatever they think. Honesty should, within the framework of feedback delivery, support the individual, and that needs to be maintained at all times. If you follow your performance management piece, and you say, "Listen, you've got ninety days to shape up or I'm going to fire you," that's not going to motivate someone who is struggling to get it right. That just puts you right at the top of their shitty leader list. You have made it about yourself, no humility, no support for the employee.

It's about honesty in feedback delivery so, "I've noticed that this isn't improving and we've talked about it in the last two coaching sessions, help me to understand what we need to do differently." That's honest and direct, and it's supportive to the individual. You just have to be aware of where honesty fits into your brand. Don't abuse that honesty and think that you can hide behind it, yet still be shitty. "Well, I don't know why he complained, because I told him the truth. I told him that he sucked. I told him that I'm going to fire him if he doesn't smarten up. I told him that I don't like how he dresses, because he looks like an idiot."

Well, how do you think you could have delivered that in a more supportive way? You'd be surprised how many people hide behind, "Well, I was honest, so you can't fault me for that." Yes, you were honest, but you were honest in a shitty way. See the difference?

WHY IS INTEGRITY IMPORTANT?

The definition of integrity I like the most is from dictionary.com:

> "Having integrity means doing the right thing in a reliable way. It's a personality trait that we admire, since it means a person has a moral compass that doesn't waver. It literally means having 'wholeness' of character, just as an integer is a 'whole number' with no fractions."

How much integrity do you display as a leader? Significantly linked to integrity is confidentiality, which is a big part of being a leader. There are certain times within the business world that you cannot divulge things. You should never discuss one employee with another employee. You should maintain confidence when people come to you. You should never gossip about your staff. You should never use company resources for personal things. If I see an employee on Facebook during the day, it makes me cringe. By all means enjoy Facebook, but not on your work computer. Create those ground rules for your own definition of integrity, and hold confidentiality as a top priority. When you erode your boss' trust, it's very hard to get it back; when you erode your employees' trust, it's almost impossible. They're not going to listen to anything you say. If you are caught talking about someone behind his or her back, it can be career suicide. It is certainly leadership suicide. I always stress the importance of confidentiality in the workplace during new leadership induction. This also includes all those things you were privy to prior to becoming a leader, for those promoted from within.

Honesty and integrity are so important when you're building your leadership brand. If you're trying to develop your brand, to become an active leader, then telling your employees what they want to hear won't work. They'll see through you in a heartbeat. You're not building credibility, and you're not branding yourself in any way other than as a liar or weak. People don't respect you, and expect you to tell them only what they want to hear. If there's a problem, you need to address it. It's your job as an active leader.

Depending upon the magnitude, you might not be able to wait until your next one-on-one, you might have to give feedback in real-time. It's creating that brand of consistency where you treat everybody with the same level of respect and fairness, even though you might approach them differently because they're all individuals. Sure, you can joke around and engage with your employees through humour, but ultimately, your job is to identify and help change behaviour for the betterment of the employee and the company.

I'll say it again, that is your job as an active leader. You can give honest feedback in a way that focuses on the employee, that helps the individual build their brand as an employee. If you focus on the employees, their performance will follow. If you focus on the numbers, you're missing the people that you need to work on in order to produce those numbers. When you focus on the data, you think you're driving data, but you forget that it's your people actually driving that data. If you're not honest about your feedback, if it doesn't link back to what you'd like your brand to be, then you're not demonstrating humility. All that you are demonstrating is ineffective shitty leadership.

A long time ago I was a manager at a company where a group of account managers who were used to being in a technical environment needed to transition to a contact centre setting. It was a new experience for them—previously they could come in at any time, and they could work from 8:00 AM to 4:00 PM or 9:00 PM to 5:00 PM. They could get up from their desk whenever they wanted. They had a portfolio of customers who they supported. A customer would call in and ask for something to be done, and they'd be able to say, "Yeah, no problem. I'll do that for you now... Done!"

The call centre that they had to move to had different rules. Now, they were going to be on a schedule, with a scheduled break and lunch, which would rotate. It was going to alternate. They had to be at their desk because they were operating on a queue system, which meant they could get a call from anyone. They now had to understand the magnitude and variances of a comprehensive range of customers. The services that they had provided in the past, they now had to charge for, based on the level of service the customers purchased, because the company was changing its strategy. That was the challenge for them, and I understood that.

Most of the account managers hated it. One of my staff members, who was double my age—I was quite young at that time—was very vocal about not liking this change. I tried to win him over; I wanted him to like me. I couldn't understand why he didn't already like me. Likeability was my motivation back then, so in our conversations, I would almost sound like I was pleading with him. In a way, I was making it about me.

Not that I said, "Why don't you like me!" But I'd ask him, "Why don't you want to do this? Why don't you listen to what I am sharing with you? Why don't you buy into this, because I can help you?" Thinking from his perspective, why would he buy into me or this new change when he didn't agree with it? "You're an idiot. Leave me alone. I don't want this change." He eventually ended up quitting and leaving the company.

Years later, reflecting on that, I realised I had perceived his reaction as one about me, and I shouldn't have. I should have been transparent and said, "Listen, here are the changes we're making. I know that some of them aren't going to be easy for you, but I want your thoughts and feedback so that we can do this together. We have to accept the fact that it's changing, because it is. If you're not happy about that, you have decisions to make, however, as we move forward, these are my expectations. If you have issues, then let's talk about them and see if we can come up with a happy medium, versus what I just need you to do."

I wasn't that honest with myself at the time though. I focused on why he didn't like me instead of what I could do to help him understand the new role and to help him try to buy into it at a level that worked for him. I did him a disservice because I made it about me. I didn't sit down and say, "Here are the pieces that are set in stone if you want to work here, and here are the pieces that we can negotiate on." Then, figure out what works for him, and perhaps see if there is another opportunity for him within the company, if this role just isn't the right thing for him. He quit and I just accepted it, "Yeah, bye. See you." I didn't do anything to stop it. I didn't do anything to help him. I wasn't being a very good leader.

THE IMPORTANCE OF HONESTY
Reflection Questions

› Reflect on a time when you have been too honest with an employee. What did you say and what would you do differently today?

› Reflect on a time when your integrity and trust in the workplace was questioned. How did that make you feel? What was the outcome?

› Think about the beginning stages of your own leadership brand. Complete the following:

   a. I prefer my leader to lead me through…

   b. I prefer to receive constructive feedback…

   c. If you want the best from me…

   d. My triggers for demotivation are…

   e. I choose to actively lead my team by demonstrating behaviours that I want my team to hold me accountable for. They are…

TRUST AND INTEGRITY

"Trust is built when someone is vulnerable and not taken advantage of."
– Bob Vanourek, author of Triple Crown Leadership

EVERYONE HAS MORAL AND ETHICAL CONVENTIONS about doing the right thing in all circumstances, even those times when no one is watching. That's how you trust yourself. What does integrity mean to you? Having integrity means you're being true to yourself, that you aren't doing things that dishonour yourself and your set of values. Integrity is about keeping those promises you've made, never betraying trust. Integrity can be found in the little things, like giving the cashier money back when they give you too much change.

Integrity also means you don't let someone else take the blame for something that you did. Integrity is building your partner up, not knocking them down. It's not taking your feelings out on someone when you've had a bad day. It's adhering to company policies. Integrity can even go as far as not taking supplies from the office. Some people don't have any issues with doing that. I'm not that much of a stickler, I would take paper if I needed some, but I'm not going to steal a stapler. I'll bring it back if I'm using it. That's just me.

Everyone has his or her own moral code. If someone else's moral code is different from yours, it doesn't automatically make him or her wrong. You need to understand where your ethical compass falls. That will dictate how you view your brand and what integrity means to you.

That's why perception management is essential. My ethical code might be vastly different from one of my peers. It doesn't necessarily make it right or wrong, or make one of us better than the other, it's just a difference. Part of perception management is learning to accept those differences as they are, because differentiation is okay. I can't work from your morals, I can't work from your leadership brand because I'm not you, and that's okay.

WHAT PEOPLE SAY BEHIND YOUR BACK IS NONE OF YOUR BUSINESS

"What others think of you is none of your business." I don't know who said it, but it's one of my favourite quotes. If someone is talking about you behind your back, what they're saying is none of your business. If people are gossiping, if people are talking about you to someone else, it wasn't meant for you to hear.

I'm a venter. I believe that everyone in the workplace should have a trusted peer that they can vent to when necessary. "I need you to talk me off the ledge for five minutes." Or, "I just need you to shut up and listen. I'm going to go on my soapbox, I'm going to sound whiny and immature, I just need to vent for a minute." For some, venting is a natural release. It's getting rid of the angst and tension that they've built up for whatever reason. From a workplace perspective, when I had a non-shitty leader, my venting requirements were always minimal. That is something to reflect on.

I tell my teams that if they want or need to vent, they can come to me because I'm a safe vent. I will never use what you vent about to your disadvantage. I will never use that against you. As long as I know you're venting, even if it was me who upset you and you want to come and vent about me, let's go for it. I've offered that opportunity to people, and they have used it because sometimes they have thought, "Wow, you really upset me. You did this, and I hated it!"

Once they're done venting I can ask them if they want to talk about it and fix it or if it was enough just to get it off their chests. That's how you change things, that is how you stop harbouring stuff, and that's how you prevent things from building up and exploding further down the road. When we choose not to vent, the pressure that builds up can lead to the manifestation of misperceptions.

It is important to make sure that when staff are venting, they make that fact known. Once, someone was venting about me to someone else. They didn't state they were venting, so the person they vented to came back and told me. Now, it was pretty harsh stuff that they were saying. I had no choice but to say something because it was going to affect our relationship. When the person told me what the other team member had said, the issue wasn't between me and the person who had vented. It was the betrayal of confidence by the individual who told me. What was their motivation? You know that communication is about intent. Why was he telling me this? I learned from that experience that when someone comes to me and says, "Well, I really shouldn't be telling you this but…" I stop them instantly and say, "Well, then why are you?"

From a leadership perspective, if you tell me something that is detrimental to the business or to an employee, I have no choice but to act on that. I won't buy into silence as consent, so when they tell me that they want to raise this with me, but that they don't want it to go to HR, then I have to say, "Well, I can't guarantee that because if you tell me something that is a code of conduct or ethical issue, I have no choice but to go to HR. I can't make that promise."

That's being honest, that's having integrity, and that's effective communication. Behaviours like these can lead to positive change and the building of trust. If instead I said, "Okay. Yes, of course, tell me," but then found myself in a situation where I had to go behind their back to get HR involved anyway, I would never earn their trust. Never make promises that you can't keep. It's better to under promise and then over deliver.

TRUST AND INTEGRITY
Reflection Questions

› Reflect on the emotional triggers that support your choices of unproductive behaviours. What are they and why?
› Reflect on your past venting sessions with someone you've trusted. What do you normally choose to vent about? Think about the reasons why and look for patterns.

THE
INTEGRATION

YOU DON'T HAVE TO LIKE ME (AND I DON'T HAVE TO LIKE YOU)

"Insult is a monstrous scorpion, and compliment is a likeable nightingale; one stings mercilessly, and the other sings sweetly."
– Mehmet Murat Ildan

THERE ARE MANY PEOPLE THAT I HAVE MANAGED, led and coached over my career who, on a personal level, I would not want to socialise with outside of the office. Does that make me a shitty leader? No! It makes me human. As leaders, we are not going to personally like everyone we support. However, that should never influence the way they are treated. It's part of my integrity and brand.

How we personally feel about someone doesn't matter, because we have become self-aware enough to know that due to our ethical code we take leadership very seriously, and it is our responsibly to support that individual just as much as we would support someone who we do like.

How do you make sure that those personal feelings don't dictate your actions? Wine? Venting? Spending time with personal friends? All good coping strategies but not always available or appropriate during work hours. The bottom line is that you've come this far in your management career and development. You've exposed yourself by showing vulnerability and by identifying how you would like to be seen and perceived as a leader. Now, you're faced with a new employee, one who—for whatever reason—you don't "like." What do you do?

You use what you've learnt so far about your trust and integrity, and most importantly, your perception management. If you roll your eyes whenever a certain individual says something, that person is eventually going to pick up on it. They're going to stop talking to you, or they're going to eventually call you out and say, "What's with the eye rolls?"

Ask yourself, what it is about the person that you don't like? Sometimes, when you ask that direct question to yourself, you will see that you don't really know why—you simply don't like them. And that's not a reason to give them any sort of sub-par treatment, especially if you are their direct manager. You have to release the dislike and make it not about you. This is a great opportunity for you to practise restrain and self-reflection. Sometimes we just don't like someone and that's okay. We don't have to like everyone. In the realm of leadership, you need to proceed extra carefully here as you'd never want them to perceive your dislike for them; they deserve all your time, attention and support just like those who you do like. The future reflections will be vast in this area and I challenge you to keep these likeability development opportunities near the top of your list.

IT'S ALL ABOUT CHOICE

Everything we do in life is a choice—from the moment we get up in the morning, to the time we go to bed. If I'm having a conversation with someone and I'm thinking, "You have really hurt my feelings," what has really happened here? They said something. It travelled out of their mouth. It came across the air, it went into my ear and my brain processed it. That took a millisecond.

At that moment, I have a choice, whether it's conscious or not. I have a choice to take the words from another person and determine how I'm going to react to them. That is my choice! If I am insecure, or I happen to be in a low period in my day, I might choose to be offended because that's where I am at that moment. Am I self-aware enough to recognise in real-time how to react or respond to communications? Or, perhaps I would choose to find it funny and laugh. Whatever it is, we make that choice. Many people forget that they have the power to choose how they react to things. We are not defined by what happens to us, we are defined by how we choose to handle it. One of my favourite quotes is from Eleanor Roosevelt.

"No one can make you feel inferior without your consent."

This equates to all kinds of basic communication, across all facets of life. Earlier this year, a woman at the Tube Station walked into me and didn't apologise. Instead, she gave me this horrible dirty look and said, "Watch where you're going!" I retorted with, "You should watch where you're going!" Without hesitation, she whips and around and said, "Okay, fatty."

She had a six or seven-year-old child with her. I asked her, "Is that the role model you want for your child?" In that moment, I had chosen to let her fat shaming bother me, and I didn't have to. I should've let it go. I'm glad I didn't swear at her; I didn't want to take the bait, because her child was present. That was certainly disgusting behaviour, and I chose to let it bother me.

Even worse, I thought about the encounter all day. I was so upset. I had dressed myself that morning about an hour earlier and I was wearing my skinny jeans, I was feeling really good about myself.

Over the last seven years I have lost over 135 kilograms. Generally, I'm confident in those kinds of situations. I've helped coach others with their own weight management, but for some reason, I chose to let it get to me. I needed to get a level of clarity in my thinking to consciously or subconsciously remember that the power of choice was within me. I took the bait and shouldn't have.

WHY IT IS IMPORTANT TO KEEP PERSONAL FEELINGS OUT OF IT

Most of us have a "tell." Experts have studied body language for years. On a first date, if someone is leaning into the other person, it shows that they're giving him or her the green light and that there is interest. If you've ever been on a first date where there's zero chemistry you'll know what I'm talking about —you can't wait to be gone, you look at your watch, you yawn, you look at your phone, and you're not making eye contact. You're disengaged. When we like people, it's easy, and we innately show it. When we don't like people, we have the same kind of tell. The same applies at work. Increase your active leadership, know your perception management, and know the shadows you cast, so that when you are engaged with someone, you are aware of whether you are truly giving them full attention, and they are aware of that, too.

Your phone is put away, you're focused on them, and you challenge yourself to remain in that positive headspace every single time you're delivering feedback or running a coaching session. If that becomes part of your leadership brand, then not divulging how you personally feel becomes easy. You are simply following your brand and integrity. You know how you want to be seen as a leader, so your personal feelings are moot.

Remember, if your staff members don't like you, you'll know it. You will be able to tell, but don't let that dishearten you. I've mentioned it before, likability shouldn't be your motivation. If you give them what they require over time, they will naturally progress towards liking you. At the very least it won't matter whether they like you or not since it's not about you, and you're seeing them improve. That is the situation you are aiming to achieve, you're on your way to becoming less shitty!

YOU DON'T HAVE TO LIKE ME
Reflection Questions

- How do you feel when you learn that some people don't like you, at work or at home? Reflect on the differences between the two scenarios and what you normally do about it in each one.

- Reflect on the concept of choice. What were your initial reactions? Reflect on the power of this concept and on times when you have chosen.

- What coping or reminder strategies will you implement to help bring you back into your leadership brand during times when you have stepped out of it?

WHAT DEMANDING RESPECT GETS YOU

"Above all, don't lie to yourself. The man who lies to himself and listens to his own lie comes to a point that he cannot distinguish the truth within him, or around him, and so loses all respect for himself and for others. And having no respect he ceases to love."
– Fyodor Dostoyevsky, The Brothers Karamazov

My father worked hard for his entire life. He wasn't much of a complainer; he went to work, did his job and supported his family. I recall when I was younger overhearing him telling my mum about his boss. He referred to her as a dragon, hot-headed and not open even *slightly* to reason or dialogue. It was her way or none at all. She enforced ten minutes of exercise a day at 11:00 am for all staff. This was non-negotiable—she demanded it and wanted no excuses. I wonder how this would be received today.

I also know of someone years ago who worked at a company where mandatory religious and bible studies were part of the weekly regime. The owners brought their personal beliefs into their company and expected everyone to participate. Everyone is entitled to their own personal beliefs, but they should not be enforced or brought into the workplace. Times sure have changed.

YES, SIR. YES, MA'AM!

In the baby boomer era, respect was demanded. It was the culture of the yes-man and yes-woman. "Yes, sir. Yes, ma'am." People would stand up at their desks when their boss walked in. That was a sign of respect, it was very military. Those days are long gone.

Thinking about your own perception management, the level-setting of your brand, your integrity, your trust, and everything we've covered so far in this book, reflect on your own level of humility and views on respect. Is this something you demand, or has it been rightfully earned?

To be a successful active leader, you have to earn respect. You earn it at an individual level by giving each of your folks what they need as an employee. Mutual genuine respect is a natural by-product of active leadership. You don't have to demand respect, because you'll inherently receive it, if you've given your staff what they need.

Similarly, you shouldn't have to force the data, because if your staff members are aligned, happy, educated, motivated, and inspired due to active and un-shitty leadership, they will ultimately want to do their best for you and the company. The right data will emerge as a natural result.

WHAT DEMANDING RESPECT GETS YOU
Reflection Questions

› Reflect on a time when you may have been accused of or perceived as demonstrating narcissistic behaviour. When, where and why do you think this was the perception? Otherwise, think about when you yourself perceived this about someone. How did it feel? Why did you perceive this?

THE EGO CONTINUUM

"The ego is only an illusion, but a very influential one. Letting the ego-illusion become your identity can prevent you from knowing your true self. Ego, the false idea of believing that you are what you have or what you do, is a backwards way of assessing and living life."
– Wayne Dyer

IMAGINE YOU'RE STANDING AT A CROSSROADS. There are two roads directly in front of you. You're standing there feeling calm, grounded, collected and certain. You're standing at your balance point—that place where you are right in the middle of your own leadership brand. Your team is aware of it and it's easy to see your alignment in what you say and do. Your balance point is where you feel the most authentic and aligned.

Standing at the crossroads, there are two different roads ahead. One is called Narcissism. One is called Insecurity. The further we travel away from our balance point down these roads, the higher the likelihood of being misperceived, depending on the road we take and other external factors.

The narcissist can be defined and perceived as a person who has an excessive interest in, or admiration of, himself or

Your balance point—where you choose "Right" or "Kind". What's your balance between narcissism and insecurity?

herself. By definition, without context, some may feel that it doesn't sound so bad. Why is that negative? In some instances, it isn't. Be cautious though, as the further down this road you travel, the more likely you are of causing counter-productive misperceptions of your leadership brand amongst your team and peers. As you begin to walk down the narcissism road, others may perceive you as determined, strong, courageous, complacent, commanding, authoritative, demanding, arrogant, vain, pushy, rude, self-righteous, pretentious—some of these words pave the road to narcissism and hypocritical behaviours that can lead to the perception of shitty leadership. These are not always accurate, but we already know this about perceptions, right?

Your leadership brand might require strength, courage and determination during some moments. These characteristics help to keep operations on track, host productive meetings or deliver clear feedback in a direct manner. These are not negative behaviours, but can be misperceived by others. Displaying these behaviours, and making certain that those involved understand why you're doing so, maintains the integrity of your leadership brand, and reduces the potential of misperceptions that can influence your team negatively.

Take a look down the other road; there you will find insecurity. Some of us tend to visit this familiar place on a daily—and sometimes hourly—basis, in some capacity. This is a place where self-doubt can rear its ugly head and cause a plethora of validation-seeking thoughts and discussions, venting and even some adult onset whining. This road can easily create victim-like behaviours, which lead to victim-like perceptions. If you've ever noticed your staff or peers rolling their eyes during one of your past self-deprecating moments, congratulations, you have now just received your day pass and clearance to travel down insecurity road.

When you're moving towards insecurity, you may be perceived as vulnerable, kind, soft, timid, anxious, negative, doubtful, uncertain, unclear, unconfident, a victim, self-loathing, self-deprecating, and self-doubting. You may coach someone who is having a hard time with a personal matter. As a non-shitty leader, you know they need reflection to help them cope, so you choose to make yourself vulnerable by sharing a personal yet professional example. Some perceive vulnerability as a weakness and can't fathom the idea of demonstrating it as a leader, never mind in the workplace. You did it to help demonstrate that vulnerability can be a positive. Others might see it as insecurity. You demonstrated that it's a sign of strength. It gave your employee what they needed, so that's a success. Remember, some may also perceive the sharing of personal reflections as "all about you," so keep that in mind when sharing so you can effectively manage the perceptions accordingly.

Perceptions occur frequently and can confuse many situations. When you identify and own your leadership brand, you are self-aware enough to know when you're using these new skills for good or when you've fallen outside your own leadership brand borders. Alternatively you simply haven't marketed your skills well enough for your staff to know your baseline balance point. When you help them to understand all of this, they will understand you and misperceptions will dramatically reduce. As your staff members learn about you through your brand, and when you become consistent, if you deviate, they not only see it, they also offer support to help guide you back to your balance point. Those moments are usually quite heartfelt and trust building.

Your ability to effectively demonstrate active leadership whilst maintaining your balance point relies on your ability to manage your individual and self-created leadership brand. Your individual brand, when published, helps your team to be aware of the leader you want to be and the leader you have told them you are. Your brand allows you to remain accountable yet true to yourself and the person you've chosen to be through active leadership. This, along with your self-awareness allows you to instantly recognise when you've become unbalanced and travelled too far down one side of the road—or down the ego-continuum—past strength, courage, determination, and into self-righteousness, leading to a perception of narcissism.

Alternatively, you've gone past venting and self-worth into self-doubt and into insecurity perceptions. Either way, when you drift too far down these roads, you should stop, recognize your surroundings, and imagine you're standing on your balance point, holding your leadership brand in both arms, like a warm

Your leadership brand zone—how do you want to be perceived?

hug, recalling all the work you've done to build your self-awareness skills, in order to return back into your leadership brand zone. Engage whatever coping strategies that you've mastered to date to help bring you back into your leadership brand zone, where you can find that inner strength to disengage the negative and replace it with the positive. This is where you're able to remain in a reasoning behavioural state. You are calm and collected. You can immediately see when to choose kind versus right, and can draw upon your own personal learning in order to help motivate and inspire others.

You can actively lead anyone, demonstrate humility and help him or her achieve his or her required behavioural changes. Why? Because of your leadership brand, your personal leadership mantra, and because of what you bring to the table as a true and active leader. That part of leadership is all about you; what you need to do now is master this, so that you always make it about them!

THE BIRTH OF THE EGO CONTINUUM

The Ego Continuum came to light whilst dealing with the most influential of shitty leaders I've ever experienced throughout my career. Instead of crawling into a hole, which at that time would have been a very safe and easy choice, I started putting my thoughts on paper.

This experience was different to the others I have shared. This was a peer; someone I didn't report to who had become a friend. She had been with the company for many, many years, in a variety of roles. She was not a senior leader, but with her great knowledge and loud boisterous presence, employees listened when she spoke. She was loud in meetings and would speak up, at times inappropriately, based on the audience. She would call out everyone's errors, shaming them in front of others. Then she'd come into my office to vent or moan about someone, only returning to be sweet and kind to their face. She was a mishmash of great humour, being personable, mean spirited and a bully—all in one. The variance in behaviour and mood contributed to the toxicity in the environment and many feared these moods.

As experienced, she chose never to take any personal or constructive feedback, in fact, she rarely wanted to hear it. If I even remotely attempted to provide something, which was always to try and help, and even soliciting permission to share, she would disengage and I'd be ignored for a few days. Upon her return, she would act like nothing happened. I chose to live with it rather than fix it, as she was a peer—and friend—rather than my true responsibility to support. I tried, but she wanted nothing, and as I opted to be kind, I let it go, didn't take it personally and accepted her as she was.

Two senior leaders approached me to take on a new role within the organisation. I was humbled. Upon reflection, it wasn't truly the career progression I wanted, but it was financially the right move at the time. Ultimately, I accepted the role and was asked to keep the news confidential, which I knew I could easily maintain. I said nothing. When the news had been revealed that I was assuming the role, I immediately received a text message, with some very inappropriate name-calling. This was from my "friend" who, after I attempted to explain my journey, wanted nothing to do with me anymore and ended our friendship. It was a sad day, but since I had experienced these emotional outbursts previously, I made the assumption that this outburst too, would pass.

Whenever our paths crossed in the corridors of work, she would avoid all eye contact, not return my "hello's," and simply ignore my very presence. The duration of this silent treatment was not typical, so after a few attempts at live contact, I sent an email. I explained what had transpired and my commitment to confidentiality, that I thought that the silent treatment was unprofessional, and that we should discuss the matter to find some common ground on which we could work together professionally. I simply wanted to understand what she was upset about. She didn't apply for this role so what was she so upset about that would end a friendship? She wasn't the least bit interested in the opportunity when it was posted, so what was her issue? I wanted to understand so I could help the situation and stop the negativity, and the staff were noticing her distance from me.

Drama between leaders is hot gossip worthy of the evening news, and it's absolutely **not** part of my brand, so I wanted it to stop. The email attempt at communication set off a series of events that were childish and immature. All I wanted was to come to work, to do my job, help make a difference and hopefully laugh a bit throughout the day. We spend a third of our life at the office, so I prefer to work in a toxic-free, simple environment where adults act like adults.

Believe me, my deep secrets are really not that exciting, however, they are mine to share. After realising the damage she was attempting to do at work through a series of events, and through sharing my personal details—some of which were exaggerated to make them sexier—I opted to take matters into my own hands and I filed a complaint. Unfortunately, the company did not follow proper protocol and the complaint was never resolved. This is a prime example of shitty leaders all in one area, running a department that is supposed to support staff. She returned to work, nothing changed, and her behaviours were permitted to continue. I had a decision to make. I made the choice to not remain a victim; I resigned, walked away and never looked back. I immediately felt a sense of relief knowing that I had made the right decision. I left frustrated, but relieved.

Prior to my departure we had a brief and civil conversation that she instigated. She spoke eloquently about how she felt the day she found out that I had got the job. She was instantly hurt that I didn't share it with her. She felt that I had chosen the company over our friendship. She felt a sense of betrayal that I didn't engage her insights and opinions in my own decision-making process. I appreciated the dialogue and understood what had happened. Her insecurities had taken over and she had chosen to feel all of the above.

I didn't make her feel that way, she chose to feel that way, and then through her lack of self-awareness, went into retaliation mode to teach me a lesson. Nothing more came of that and we never spoke again. My epiphany came later that day. I had convinced myself she was a complete drama queen narcissist, that she truly thought she was better than most. I thought she was riddled with entitlement that she couldn't believe that I would choose a direct order of confidentiality from two senior leaders over our friendship, but that sharing personal and confidential details from my life was acceptable. I had been misreading her behaviours incorrectly the entire time. She wasn't high and mighty; she was self-doubting and lacking complete self-awareness. By engaging in bullying, mean-spirited behaviours, she kept people away. They couldn't get too close simply because they didn't want to, and she made sure of that by the way she conducted herself. It was clear to me that most perceived narcissistic behaviours are not really narcissistic at all, they are an outward sign of insecurity. Reflect on that for a moment, how many people do you know who have demonstrated these behaviours?

One of the many unfortunate components of this story is that her behaviours made her a look like a shitty leader. Staff were intimidated by her and scared of her. They disliked her communications style, her outward disrespect when shaming staff in front of others, and her inability to take any constructive feedback. The company long before my arrival knew these behaviours yet they chose to do nothing to help her. She is a prime example of how silence is consent and a by-product of working for, in this case, a toxic organisation with shitty senior leaders who simply breed incompetence through their own inability to see how narcissistic their behaviours make them appear.

The truth is, in fact, the exact opposite. These people are not egocentric, and the company has great potential, even though they, and the majority of their leaders are perceived to be below

Crossing out of your leadership brand zone into the land of misperceptions.

standard active leaders. They are riddled with insecurities, self-doubt and a complete lack of self-awareness which means that they are unable to recognise the trail of toxicity they leave behind. That is insecurity, not ego.

The Ego Continuum is a means to help both organisations and their staff to better understand the value of their true self, and their self-truth. Ego is defined as the false self.

When standing at a crossroad, you always have a choice—you have to choose a direction. If one of the paths is labelled "right," and the other, "kind," which do you choose?

In my last story, when I was experiencing my own personal challenges, the day I came home after making the decision to leave the company I stumbled across a television show on PBS where Deepak Chopra was talking about the power of choice. It was one of those kismet moments where it seemed that I was just where I was meant to be. I never turn on PBS, ever. I was home from a really shitty day spent dealing with the shitty behaviours of people who were shitty leaders. I turned my TV on and my cat accidentally changed the channel to PBS. There was clearly a higher purpose wanting me to see this, and the timing could not have been more perfect. Deepak was talking about choosing to be either right or kind. It stayed with me for two years. From that moment, and on the reflections of twenty-five years of leadership coaching, the Ego Continuum began.

When we feel the need to be right in order to prove our point to others, what is that really saying about us? Do you argue with friends, family and co-workers? Do you find that when you argue, you're passionate about wanting to be right? Why is being right so important to you? If you're arguing with a partner, why is it so important for you to be right? Or why is it that you want them to be wrong?

If we choose kind, instead of right, we let go of the unnecessary. Simply being in the moment and choosing an honest path, what can that do for our own thoughts, feelings, and well-being?

RIGHT VS KIND IN MY PERSONAL LIFE

Sometimes, however, people don't make it easy to choose being kind over being right, and we have to really call on our own courage to do so. If this was easy, people would do it all the time and there would be no need for books like this.

As a single gay man approaching fifty, I have chosen online dating in an attempt to meet a possible future partner. In the past I have travelled a similar road, and can reflect on times when I chose the validation of others over my own thoughts and feelings. This certainly wasn't a healthy experience at the time, and I can now reflect on improving my approach to cyber dating. As a result, it has now become more fun, enlightening and sometimes a comical, yet eye-rolling experience.

I started chatting with a certain gentleman. We hit it off, and there was an instant chemistry and connection. We had a couple of dates and they were lovely. As we progressed into our discovery, a couple of things were not adding up. I started feeling a little uncomfortable with some of the stories he was choosing to share in regards to his close friends, revealing things that were none of my business, and clearly things his friends had shared in confidence. It was starting to leave a bitter aftertaste. I determined that after a very fast moving nine days, and two dates, we were not a good fit.

We had a quick phone conversation. I avoided the "it's not you, it's me" approach, I simply explained that I didn't feel we were a good match and left it there. We parted amicably as adults who have had two dates should.

A few hours later I received an email. It was a rather scathing email where he chose to provide his personal and unsolicited opinions about my character, personality and physical attributes. A few lines into the email, when I read the words, "you're still fat," I saw myself at my own crossroads. Instantly, right versus kind kicked in. I felt all positive attributes connected to my own leadership brand flying out the window. I was standing in the dark, dank wasteland riddled with those feelings of insecurity and self-doubt.

I was standing at a crossroads struggling to remain balanced. Do I choose right or do I choose kind? Do I click reply and start spewing off all of the worst four-letter words I could think of? Do I say, "How dare you send me this email? I am so offended." Or do I simply read it, hit delete, and move on with my life?

Outside our leadership brand—do you know when it's time to turn back?

I chose kind. I chose to maintain my composure and to stop reading mid-email. It didn't mean anything as it was meant to hurt me. His unsolicited opinions were not relevant enough for me to engage in any remote interest of allowing his words to enter my brain. The receiving end of a scathing email was not where I wanted to be. I spared him, and more importantly, I spared myself. It wasn't worth the time and effort of retaliation because it didn't matter to me what he thought.

I just deflected everything he said because it wasn't worth the time or energy to vent to my close friends about what had happened. As a self-proclaimed venter, I knew that every time I recalled the story, I would live through it again. I wanted to spare my friends this too.

Even with my weight loss success, my biggest personal insecurity is still my current weight and the areas of my body that I'm not pleased with, which are still a work in progress. In the past, whenever someone made a personal attack on my weight, it was always self-destructing. This time, I chose to not engage, I chose kind over right and let it go. This was a new experience for me, and one I personally felt worthy of sharing with you here. Personal growth can manifest itself sometimes in places where we least expect it.

RIGHT VS KIND IN MY PROFESSIONAL LIFE

I was working as a consultant for a company where I had two managers who were both not as effective in leadership as they could have been. They had been working in a culture where they were steady Eddy's—they came into work, did what they needed to do in order to get by, didn't offer much that was over and above, but enough to maintain their value. They rarely received feedback of any kind so they just assumed they were doing their jobs well. When they did receive feedback it was not delivered with the intent of benefitting their development. Their staff members, who weren't reflective enough to see past regular day-to-day behaviours, enjoyed them because they were likeable and fun.

It is near impossible to teach people how to become self-aware when they are stuck in their own narcissism and insecurity, rut or challenges. There were times when I was coaching them that I chose to be right instead of kind because of my own frustrations, when I felt that I was just spinning my wheels on an icy road. They were missing deadlines, refusing to perform tasks in meetings, and they were over-complicating matters with their staff. They would hold onto things, lacking the ability to delegate. They weren't being honest with feedback, or taking advantage of the opportunities afforded to them by having someone who wanted to help them achieve greater results through self-awareness, and by recognising their own Ego Continuum.

Eventually they both moved on to other roles within the company. They weren't ready to hear or accept feedback. They left because of a combination of their own pride and because for years they had worked for an organisation that lacked a feedback culture that didn't support the truth. They became a product of their environment. I exonerate them from some of their actions. In fairness, they both did show improvements closer to the end of our time together which I was very pleased to witness. Ultimately, when your senior leaders are uninspiring and do not understand the importance of a feedback culture, or simply choose to dismiss its value, it will eventually take its toll on your line managers. Change then seems futile, your staff enter self-preservation mode, and the shittiness ensues. It sounds bleak because it is. Even the best leaders wouldn't remain in this type of environment for long.

As a leader, you can only be kind so many times before you have to choose to be right. The key is always to be aware of where you are. The "right" versus "kind" challenge is about keeping your own level of self-awareness and ego in check. Where are you on the Ego Continuum at this moment? I'm feisty and I want to be right, so be careful of what you say to me? Or am I willing to let go and be kind? Have I just been stuck in a three-hour traffic delay? Have I spilled my coffee, has a dog bit my leg, or has my wife left me? I'm in a bad mood right now so the last thing in my head is being kind to you.

Again, these are not excuses for being a shitty leader. If you're a leader and you're showing humility, you can separate your personal life, go into work and give your staff what they need because you know it's not about you—it's about them. If, at this point, you are ready to make a positive step towards really understanding who you are, how you communicate, how you think, how you process information, how you make choices, how you're perceived by others, the shadows you cast, what your leadership brand is, then we can get to the real truth of washing away your low self-worth, or your fears, and progress forward into achieving real passion.

True happiness is defined through effective choices illuminating in your life what the soul seeks for fulfilment, where your inner passions are hosted and fed as they are meant to be. You feel your soul's hunger every day. How hungry are you?

THE EGO IN CONVERSATION

The dictionary defines ego as a person's sense of self-esteem or self-importance. It's the psychoanalytic part of the mind that mediates between the conscious and the unconscious; it is responsible for reality testing and a sense of personal identity. "Ego" in the English language is a noun, yet when you hear people talk about ego, they refer to it with much more passion or disdain, depending upon their chosen mood at that time—giving ego a much more abstract description than just a noun.

The ego reflects so much more than just a simple noun—a person, place or thing. It represents people's fears, thoughts, judgments, and reflections. When we reflect at a mass-human level, ego as a person's sense of self-esteem or self-importance may be skewed to either one side or the other, because so many people have mastered the art of lying to themselves. How do we stop this cycle?

Self-worth, self-confidence, self-esteem, these self-identifiers are all very important, yet at times very hard to identify and master. From my own personal experiences, anything self-related has to come from within. No one dictates how you feel. No one can make you feel inferior without your consent. No one can make us feel anything, anything we choose to feel comes from inside of us.

The ego links back to communication. As mentioned earlier, within basic spoken communication there are two players, the giver and the receiver. The giver speaks words, the information flies through the air from the giver's mouth and is collected by the receiver's ear. The brain then works its magic and the receiver processes it. At that moment, there is a comprehension of what has been said, which takes in not only the words but the tone, the context, and the relationship between those two. A final decision on how to think, feel, or respond is subconsciously made by the receiver in a millisecond.

Self-awareness, self-esteem, and self-confidence play their part during this arc of the communication. If the giver says something that could upset or offend the receiver, at that moment the receiver can choose how they feel and how to respond. Words flying through the air from mouth to ear don't hurt us. You don't feel words rush past your head or slap you in the face as they're travelling through the air. We choose how to feel and think based on what others say. If we choose to believe what they have said over believing how we actually feel about ourselves, the hurt manifests. The self-doubt or lack of self-awareness takes over.

If it's a true statement and I'm not living in my false self, if I'm aware of my whereabouts on the Ego Continuum, then when someone calls me out on my own silliness, I can simply turn

Where insecurity and narcissism converge—are you so deep down either path that you're in the misperception zone?

around without any form of stress or falseness, and reply, "Yeah, you know what, you're right."

Think about past communications, specifically times when someone said something that really upset you. Reflect on why you got upset. Was it what they said that made you choose that reaction? The power of choice is a hard concept for some to grasp and to really comprehend the true value and the benefit of it. It's something that you have always had, that you will always have, and that no one can ever take away from you. We forget, for whatever reason, that we have this power of choice in the first place. Why is that? Is it cultural? Is it societal? Is it our own behaviours? Do we purposely choose to relinquish this control in order to please others? Do we even know we've done this?

In my personal and business coaching practice, time and time again I have witnessed the surprised look on the faces of those realising they had the power of choice all along. These moments of epiphany are the start of a journey of self-discovery that leads to an improved self-worth, a clearer ability to self-reflect, and a true discovery of who you really are. What are your true personal and business needs? How can you best interact with your team, and demonstrate active leadership? If you are in that leadership role, how can you identify areas of improvement so that you can lead and inspire your team to great success?

WHERE ARE YOU ON THE EGO CONTINUUM?

Your own ability to self-reflect is required from an honest perspective in order to embark on this Ego Continuum journey of self-improvement for lasting change. If you're going to lie to yourself, then you're going to stay in the false sense of self. If you're not willing to let that ego go, then it's probably not the right time to continue.

If you're truly not happy with the situation, then this may be your tipping point for change. If you'll allow me to begin on a personal level, throughout many stages of my own life and career, I have been referred to as narcissistic, conceited, arrogant, and full of myself. I have experienced what I like to call high self-confidence times in my life. These are the times when I feel really good about myself, based on a number of contributing factors such as career success, my weight loss and transformation, social activities, relationships, and even something as silly as just having a good hair day. Regardless of the reasons, I was comfortable at my balance point with a slight lean towards the narcissism side of the Ego Continuum. When people hover around this area, those who are on the insecurity side may often misconstrue confidence for conceit. They are experiencing things at that moment that prevent them from seeing confidence as a positive in others. They're unable or unwilling to see the positive because they are in a negative place or having negative thoughts. Keep in mind, the negative disposition of a person can be the result of a single moment in time. A single interaction with a person, or something as basic as waking up in a bad mood, and they may choose to let it ruin their entire day. It can also be something as simple as a stranger calling you fat.

If people breathe deeply, relax, reflect, review, have a coffee, they can alter how they feel and begin having a better day. It's really about becoming self-aware so that you recognise when you're causing your own funk. As you read, confidence can be—and often is—misconstrued as conceit by people who are feeling insecure or choosing insecurity. If we look at the concept of self-doubt, do you often find yourself questioning what you do? Do you often question your own thoughts? Do you reject people when they compliment you? "That's a really nice shirt, I like it." "Oh, this old thing? Please..."

I just gave you a compliment but instead of showing humility, you reject the compliment. It makes us uncomfortable that someone just said something nice about us, because we're in a low self-esteem mood so we're not ready to believe or accept it.

MY SISTER, THE SAINT

Like any younger sibling, when I was a kid I idolised my sister who is four and a half years older than me. To me, she had this angelic halo, that surrounded her at all times. Everyone around her loved her. She had an outstanding work ethic,

Arial view of our leadership brand and misperceptions zone.

and she applied herself wholeheartedly to everything she did. She showed compassion and support to people around her, and never succumbed to the typical adolescent peer pressure bullshit that so many of us endured. I don't think she was overly confident, but she always appeared to me not to care about what other people thought of her, which I was always envious of.

Back in the day, I felt both envious and jealous, although at the time I wouldn't have known the difference. There were times when I thought I didn't like her because of that envy and negativity. There was a part of me that wanted to be more like her, and wanted people to feel about me the way they felt about her. I was much more impressionable back then and I cared what my peer group thought.

I was a creative child, with an active imagination. I put my parents through it a few times, hung out with the wrong crowd, experimented, and acted up at school. I was the class clown, because my funny accolades at least provided me with the peer acceptance I longed for as a child. My mistake was that I compared myself to my sister. I could never have been like her in any way as we're quite different people; we bring various qualities to the table. I couldn't do anything like some of what she does and nor could she do what I was good at. Here's the good part—that's completely okay because it's just doesn't matter.

We should only ever compare ourselves against ourselves. Again, I think Deepak expressed this point the most clearly, although I am sure others have over the years, too. There is no valid basis of comparison when we compare ourselves against someone else. Did I have a better day today than I did yesterday? That's the effective question to answer when comparing, just like you did during your active leadership interactions. Ask and remind yourself of what you spoke about during the last session. What is worthy of raising again, and how has it changed or improved? See how this all fits?

I absolutely adore my sister. She is strong, determined, and inspires me often to laugh in the face of adversity. She shows me that we are not defined by our failures—they are simple reminders to help get us back on track. Now, if you ever get on an airplane with her, don't have her lead the way to help you find your seat, but in all other areas, she's your rock star! (Of course there had to be at least one inside family joke, right?).

I continued along this path for many years, both in school and in employment, focusing on being the funny guy. I was hiding behind my insecurities and using it as leverage to get people to like me. It provided the attention and validation from others that I thought I needed whilst being enough of a barrier to keep people away from my truth.

That was my first thought about self-reflection and hiding behind the ego, that false self. I chose to identify as the class clown in order to avoid people getting too close. People don't generally confide in the funny ones, so I didn't have to get too close to people. I could get away with things that other people wouldn't necessarily have got away with because, "Mark's just being funny." I also had quite an active imagination as a child, often fantasising about living in a movie or that I was on TV. In short, I fantasised about reality TV twenty years before its inception. Surely there should be some royalties for that, no? Okay.

I remember during my elementary school years I told a group of girls that a family member was a Hollywood producer and that twenty of them would be spending the summer in Hollywood being extras in a movie. I liked making people feel excited and the attention I received was heavenly. Unfortunately, my parents received some phone calls asking when the flights to Hollywood departed so my gig was up. I knew my popularity time was coming to an end and I would soon be hearing, "What have you done this time Marky?" from my parents. Oh, the imagination of my child self.

If I wrote a letter to him—my 1979 elementary school, overly insecure, childlike self—helping him to understand what society and life would be like thirty years later, I would tell him not to change a thing. I would tell him to make his stories more elaborate. I would have done more of them and I would have laughed about the idiocy of it all. I wouldn't tell him to change that part of his free-spirited behaviours because they lead to this moment today. I don't know who I would have become if my parents had inadvertently been the type to stifle creativity and imagination. If they had, I may have been writing a completely different book.

Of course, if my creative imagination hurt anyone's dream of becoming a Hollywood legend, I will gladly use this forum to publicly apologise. However, should I ever sell the rights to make "Ego Continuum" – The Movie, I will absolutely circle back to those Lescon Public School peers and offer them all roles as extras. So, even after thirty-eight years, either I am still a creative, imaginative, free-thinker, or just really a nutter who's completely full of it—you decide, I support either!

THE EGO CONTINUUM
Reflection Questions

› Develop three ways you can use to choose kind versus right as you embark on your own Ego-Continuum journey.

› Review the Ego-Continuum, look at some of the key words your leadership brand could be representing. Upon initial review, what stands out the most for you and why?

› Define how narcissism and insecurity are similar.

› How does self-awareness influence your leadership brand?

INSIGHTS INTO YOUR OWN EGO CONTINUUM

"Most misunderstandings in the world could be avoided if people would simply take the time to ask, "What else could this mean?"
– Shannon L. Alder

HOW MUCH REFLECTION HAVE YOU BEEN ENGAGING in during your reading? How are you going to engage in active leadership? Do you have inputs towards creating your own leadership brand?

Take stock every morning, or before a one-on-one, a coaching session or a disciplinary meeting, even before regular interactions when you're walking through the hallways at work. How are you coming across? What's your perception? The best and easiest way to find that out is to use the Ego Continuum as your scale, as your personal self-awareness identifier. If you're having a good hair day, there's nothing wrong with self-confidence because you feel you look good. How are you coming across to people who are more insecure? If you're walking high because of positive things in your life, how are you showing that to others, and more importantly, how are they seeing it?

When you are on a personal high and you talk about the things that are good in your life right now, you're normally saying it from a point of truth. You're not saying it in a boastful way, "Look at me, look how much better I am than you." You may be simply talking about these things because you're excited about your life and you want to live it. You're excited about things that are going on and you want to share them with people. How do people perceive what you're telling them? The receivers in your conversations will formulate their thoughts based on the perceptions of your outputs that they will identify as their inputs—and what they think of you.

We know communication is about intent. *Why are you telling me this information?* Put your leadership hat on, now you're talking to one of your direct reports. How they think is very important, and is based on the way you communicate and your intent during that communication. If I have a relationship with one of my colleagues and we're not close but we get along, we respect each other but I don't generally engage in sidebar conversations with her, then we would generally keep it business ninety percent of the time.

I might be on such a high, I just want to tell everybody about how I love being single and that I have a date next weekend, for example. If I want to go into all this personal stuff with someone who doesn't know me well, who I don't normally engage with, who might be in a very different place to me, how are they going to perceive my excitement? With, "Why are you telling me all this? You're so high on yourself. I don't care. That's great for you, but I really don't care." Know your audience, know who you're communicating with, and recognise, too, that there's a time and a place for everything.

The journey to becoming a less shitty leader, towards self-awareness, begins now. What are we waiting for? Let's start.

Read the following self-awareness questions. Find yourself in your happy place, wherever that is for you. Be prepared to answer these questions 100 percent honestly. Don't waffle and don't lie to yourself. If you're not ready to be 100 percent truthful, then hold off until you're ready. This will help you to identify, based on how you feel at this moment, when you land on the Ego Continuum, and it will help you to learn what you can do about it.

YOUR GUIDE TOWARDS SELF-AWARENESS

With a partner, get each other to answer the following questions. Be smart, understand your audience, and ask if you don't understand them, as you may be providing constructive feedback. Will you choose right or kind? How honest will you be? You may learn some new insights into yourself, about the way you receive feedback, and about how truthful you are in sharing your true thoughts and insights. Are you self-aware and actively leading enough to play this authentically? How much alignment is there between your results and your leadership brand? Reflect on all insights.

With your partner, ask each other the following questions. You can write down your answer or just have a conversation. You may want to audio record your session, but make sure both parties agree. This way you can use the feedback reflectively.

› What leadership skills do I actively demonstrate?

› How do you perceive me as a leader?

› What habits/behaviours/traits do I have that you notice often? Are these positive; areas of improvement; or both?

› What do I do better than you?
› Name one key area in which you think I should improve.

You can also use these questions to poll your staff. For more insights into these questions and what you can do next, visit our website at www.ego-continuum.co.uk

INSIGHTS INTO YOUR OWN EGO CONTINUUM
Reflection Questions

› Reflect on a time when you feel that you failed an employee. What was the situation? What made you reflect on this specific issue? How did you fail them? What would you now do differently?

YOUR LEADERSHIP EPITAPH

"I could die for you. But I couldn't, and wouldn't, live for you."
– Ayn Rand, The Fountainhead

It should be stated that you are going to self-reflect on your own mortality. If you're not in the right head space to do that, based on personal circumstances, such as the loss of a friend, a partner, a parent, a loved one, an animal, this might not be the right time for you to self-reflect in this area. You need to be in a comfortable state of mind to engage in this chapter. Thank you.

YOUR EPITAPH

As a leader, we've talked about the shadows you cast, we've talked about self-awareness and active leadership, and we've talked about the Ego Continuum. This next chapter is a game you can play with anyone: peers, colleagues, anyone who is ready to delve into some deep and honest self-awareness. This requires honesty and courage. It requires the courage to say what might never have been said before, or what might never have been heard. The mortality component brings forth a level of vulnerability that, once accepted, allows participants to reveal some potential key areas that they may have been blocking or guarding for their own protected reasons.

Ask yourself, "When I die, how do I want to be remembered as a leader?" What would you say? What is the permanent shadow you want to cast for those you have supported throughout your career? What is your legacy?

No-one on his or her deathbed says, "Gee, I wish I had spent more time at the office." If you're in a leadership role, sometimes you work too hard. Sometimes you may have regrets about the past that can come up during this exercise. It's not about that. It's not about beating yourself up, saying, "I neglected my children." Or, "I didn't treat my wife as well as I should have. I gave her the lifestyle she wanted because I made £250,000 a year." When someone is faced with their own mortality, the thing they are running short of, is time. That's what makes this a challenge.

This exercise, if participation is authentic, forces you to release the ego. Simply put, how do you want to be remembered? "Oh, I wish that I could be known as the most inspirational leader." How? Why? If you're willing to play, in my past experiences here, I have seen people both struggle to find it and identify them quickly. Ask yourself if you're really ready and willing to play.

Most people, when they think about what they want as their Leadership Epitaph, find that they're not as ahead in their thinking as they thought. Some have discovered they're not as self-aware as they imagined. They're not able to articulate what they want to be remembered as, and they find it hard to come to terms with the fact that they might not be representing the brand they want to. Nobody wants to identify their brand and come to the conclusion that they are a shitty leader. It's hard for people to digest. Some people truly feel that vulnerability is a sign of weakness, even failure.

Dr. Brené Brown is my unsung hero; she has changed my life in many ways. Dr. Brown hosted a TED Talk in 2010 on vulnerability, and if you are stuck on your leadership epitaph, perform a web search. Her talk is so eye opening; she talks about how we numb the fear and the pain. When you numb fear and pain, you also numb joy, and you acclimate as a result. People wonder why they feel like robots, why they feel dead inside. It's because they are so caught up in their own fear of wanting to be right and their fear of their own stuff, that they don't realise they're numbing their happiness at the same time. That only happens when you're not self-aware.

After you've watched that TED Talk, ask yourself, what does vulnerability mean to me? What's the first thing you think of when you hear the word vulnerability? Most people say fear. I've worked with people who have said, "If I showed vulnerability in the work environment that I used to work in, I would have been fired because vulnerability is seen as a weakness." I see it as strength. If vulnerability was a weakness—something that I would get fired for if I demonstrated it—then that's not a company I would ever work for.

If you struggle to write your leadership epitaph on your own, try this exercise with a trusted peer. Try writing each other's first. This way you spark the dialogue through perceptions and that can help take the conversation to a different level of engagement.

Once you've asked the question about how you'd like to be remembered, socialise your results with your trust groups. Ask them to comment, share and reflect on their thoughts regarding your feedback. Do you all have the courage to ask challenging and reflective questions in order to develop some actionable activities to help you achieve your individual desired goals?

Once you have reflected on how you'd like to be remembered and perhaps done some investigations into your thoughts on vulnerability, you're ready to summarise the epitaph that will be carved into your leadership tombstone. This statement will define you as the leader you've chosen to be.

For more information regarding the leadership epitaph or to engage with us to help you lead this exercise within your organisation, visit us at www.ego-continuum.co.uk

YOUR LEADERSHIP EPITAPH
Reflection Questions

› If you watched the vulnerability TED Talk with Dr. Brené Brown, what were your initial reflections on vulnerability?

YOUR CORPORATE CULTURE

"Respect is how to treat everyone, not just those you want to impress."
– Richard Branson

WHAT'S THE CULTURE LIKE IN YOUR COMPANY? Usually, if I'm going into a company as a consultant, I'll ask that question immediately. Most people don't know what it means. Most people are confused. They talk about how the employees feel. "What's the culture here?" They'd reply, "Oh, yeah, people like it here." That's great, but what are the corporate values? What are your visions? Do the employees at all levels know those values? Do those employees emulate and articulate those values? Are there mass contradictions in the values?

Most companies I have worked for cite their vision and values, yet very few leaders demonstrate them consistently. It's really about understanding what company culture means, then being able to live and articulate it. Does your culture promote feedback? Does your culture uphold integrity? Does your culture perpetuate shitty leaders or do you do something about them? Do you know what to do with them? Does your culture put your employees first over your customers? When you put the customer first, you may be forgetting about your employees, and you need your employees to deal with your customers. When you put your employees first they will automatically help the customer because you're helping them. It's simple, really.

What is your company's culture? What do you think it is? What do you want it to be? Do the people at the same leadership level as you emulate your vision and values, so that when staff look up, they see it? Employees always look up to see what "good" looks like. If all they see are shitty leaders, what does that tell them about their company? That defines your culture.

When I ask, what is culture—is that a thing? Is that tangible? Can you touch it? Can you smell it? Can you taste it? What is the culture? People have a hard time answering these questions.

At 3:00 AM on a Sunday when your site is empty and everyone is at home, what's the culture like? The culture is the people. We, as leaders, set the tone for the culture. If we are a group of shitty leaders who think only about ourselves, who completely don't care about our staff or if we're perceived as not caring about our staff, because all we do is talk about ourselves, we will promote a shitty corporate culture. We don't demonstrate humility, we don't support the power of choice, and we never give people a voice or platform to speak their mind. We don't ask how they like to be led or how they like to receive feedback, so we deliver a cookie-cutter approach that does nothing. No results, no change. We wonder why profits are down, customers are leaving, and why we have high attrition. It all starts from the top; it starts from the leaders. If you don't want a shitty company culture, don't be a shitty leader.

If your company culture is shitty and you don't know how to fix it, even after you've read this book, hire someone to perform an audit top-down across your management team and your senior leaders. Together we go through a full day or two-day course and we get people actively leading. We trickle that down throughout the entire organisation and you watch the magic happen.

There's no other way for it to happen other than starting from the top down, because the top is where the decisions are made when things turn shitty. It's where the people-engagement initiatives are born and die. These are the decision-makers who believe that answering the phone faster is more important than the employee development and feedback. The culture must be there, the support must be there, active leadership must be seen as non-negotiable. You can't piecemeal your shittiness. You can't be a good leader when it suits you. You have to be un-shitty all the time. You can't pick and choose when you're a shitty leader to suit your senior level leaders. That's not how it works, and that's why behaviours and outputs don't change.

WHAT A SHITTY CULTURE LOOKS LIKE

Shitty leadership leads to a culture of apathy and disengagement, and this is what most companies I have visited in the world look like. When you, your friends and family go to work, how many times do you hear or say, "I don't want to go to work today." Why do they feel that way? Why is it there are some days when you absolutely love your job, and other days you can't stand the thought of it? Usually, people are involved, or you work in a culture that is not supportive or demanding of strong leadership.

In these shitty cultures, you will see employees who don't care. You'll sense apathy. You'll sense disengagement. You'll sense people taking longer for their breaks and lunches. You'll see high levels of sick leave, you'll see high attrition. You'll see people who don't have a purpose because they don't feel supported or aligned, and they don't believe that they're being held accountable, because when you're a good leader, you inspire people to follow the rules. When there are no rules being upheld, people will take liberties, because they simply don't care. They don't feel they have to. There's no recourse.

YOUR CORPORATE CULTURE
Reflection Questions

› How does your current corporate culture affect your leadership brand? What are you going to do about it?

› What immediate steps are you going to take to ensure you become less of a shitty leader?

CONCLUSION

"It's only after you've stepped outside your comfort zone that you begin to change, grow, and transform."
– Roy T. Bennett

When you become self-aware, when you understand your leadership brand, when you understand the shadows you cast, when you take on perception management, when you manage your staff through active leadership, when you ask how they like to be led, and how they like to receive feedback, then you promote those values you chose as your leadership brand most of the time. When you don't, you take on the accountability of those who are affected by it. When you promote and adopt everything you've read so far in this book, through natural evolution, you are on your way to becoming less of a shitty leader.

If you follow those steps, adopt them into practice, and you are actually there for your folks as a humble leader, inspiring them and giving them what they need, the shittiness reduces or goes away. Imagine what would happen if eighty percent of the leaders in any organisation in any industry were deemed not shitty? How would this impact the culture?

When you are aware of who you are and you live an authentic life, things start to change for the better. People talk about stepping outside your comfort zone, but I say you don't have to step outside your comfort zone—just make your comfort zone bigger. Expand the zone. When you are aligned and you are living from an authentic place, your self-esteem and confidence skyrocket because you feel as though you are who you are meant to be. If you read this book reluctantly at first, but now have a few tips you can start putting into practice, then congratulations—you've just expanded your comfort zone.

When you are in that place, everything we've talked about in this book becomes easier—the power of choice, not taking the bait when someone calls you fat when you've lost 135 kilograms and it's still a sensitive issue. You don't care about the mundane and the trivial because all you want to do is live your life helping other people. You have a smile on your face when you wake up, and you have a smile on your face when you go to bed. When you're in that zone of self-awareness and truth, you realise that there are no failures. There are just experiences that help remind you of who you are, who you choose to be and who you can become. It becomes contagious.

If you are reading this book as a leader, it's about being the best leader you can be so that you can reach the highest level of job fulfilment, knowing that you're making a difference in the lives of others. When you take leading seriously, you are not only affecting the lives of your staff in their career, but you're also affecting their lives outside of work. When that happens, you've created a loyal group of people who want nothing more than to help make you successful, as well as their customers and their company, because you're all aligned. Everyone is on the same page, moving towards the goal. And that's golden. That is when we love our jobs, we love what we do, and we genuinely care about each other and want to do more to ensure that it always stays this way.

NEXT STEPS

If you've realised that you might be exhibiting the behaviours of a shitty leader, or that you aren't leading as actively as you could be, the first step is to write yourself a letter. I challenge you to write a letter of honesty and truth to your former self, recognising the aspects that made you a shitty leader. You need to own it, you need to acknowledge it, and then you need to apologise for it. Writing this letter can be a very cathartic experience, it can be emotional. Then, go to a place where you can safely burn the letter so that it goes away for good. Forgive yourself—it's a thing of the past. Take a fresh start, move forward and pat yourself on the back for taking the first step. There is no need to keep beating yourself up for past mistakes. That is the beauty of self-awareness. Once you've recognised it and owned it, you can resolve it and truly move on.

Write that letter, own the shitty parts. Identify the pieces that resonated with you from this book. From this, create your plan to engage. What two things are you going to do differently tomorrow to demonstrate that you no longer want to be a shitty leader?

The initial challenge is not to tell your staff that you're doing it, just do your two things and watch what happens. If you were to say to them, "I just want to let you know I'm making these changes because I want to be a better leader," that in itself can be deemed narcissistic. It makes you look like you want validation for what you should have been doing anyway. Don't tell people you're doing it, just do it and watch what happens.

For most leaders, the first step is removing the cookie-cutter approach. "Hey, listen, I have this new idea that I wanted to talk to you about. I'm going to ask you a few questions in your one-on-one today. I want to know how you like to be led and I want to know how you like to receive feedback." If people ask why, just say, "I'm trying to become better. I want to make a difference. I want to see how this works."

When we began this journey over a hundred pages ago, I identified that people themselves are not shitty, that sometimes our behaviours are. I have shared and reflected on several personal stories to help you reflect and self-identify any of your own leadership behaviours within yourself you want to change. I don't belittle or dislike the people in these stories. I thank them, wholeheartedly and sincerely. It's their experiences that helped me to experience my own, which in turn was my catalyst and motivation in wanting to share, in the hope that this will help you to become less of a shitty leader and more of the worthy active leader we all have deep inside, just waiting to be born. Together, we can make the workplace a truly remarkable and inspired place to be.

YOUR HOW-TO GUIDE

- Practice the art of effective feedback delivery. Use the two questions. Pay attention. Make these sessions all about them. Plan what you'd like to achieve together. Have a discussion and learn things about each other. Progressive behavioural discussions focusing on improvements.

- After three/four sessions solicit feedback about your feedback delivery. Ask your staff and see what they share. Watch and reflect on how you receive it.

- Remember humility, and remember that it's no longer about you!

- Create your own leadership brand, own it and share it.

- Challenge yourself to truly become self-aware in all aspects of your life.

- Reflect on where you are on The Ego-Continuum – narcissism and insecurity lead to the same place – what shadows do you cast?

- Identify and reflect on your leadership epitaph.

- Where are you going next as you continue to un-shittify your leadership skills?

  Welcome to the Ego-Continuum. Let the non-shitty leadership movement begin!

  For additional information and support for you and your organisation on active leadership, please contact The Ego-Continuum at www.ego-continuum.co.uk

ABOUT THE AUTHOR

Mark Robinson is the creator of *The Ego-Continuum*, a how-to guide for shitty leaders to become less shitty through active leadership. Join the global non-shitty leadership movement through a building a complete awareness of the links between shitty leadership, active leadership, effective feedback and corporate culture.

With his expertise as a reformed shitty leader and a certified professional coach, Mark has personally led and coached thousands of individuals, working with top companies in North America, Asia and the United Kingdom.

To find out more about Mark, visit www.ego-continuum.co.uk

Printed in Great Britain
by Amazon